# ESCAPE FROM PANNONIA*

## A Tale of Two Survivors

* Situated in the fertile basin of the Danube and protected by the great arc of the Carpathian Mountains, Pannonia was the name of the province guarding the northeastern frontier of the Roman Empire. After the Empire hit the dustbin of history, it became the stopover point for migrating barbaric tribes: the Huns, the Avars, the Tartars, etc. From the Russian steppes, horsemen of the Magyar tribes arrived at the end of the 9th century and stayed. From the time of their arrival, Pannonia has been called Hungary.

# ESCAPE FROM PANNONIA

## A Tale of Two Survivors

**Steve Floris**

Creative Connections Publishing

National Library of Canada Cataloguing in Publication Data
Floris, Steve, 1920-
Escape from Pannonia : a tale of two survivors

ISBN 1-894694-03-1

1. Floris, Steve, 1920- . 2. World War, 1939-1945—Conscript
labor—Hungary. 3. Holocaust survivors—Biography. 4. World War,
1939-1945—Personal narratives, Hungarian. 5. Hungarian Canadians—
Biography. I. Title.

D811.5.F58 2001      940.53'17'092      C2001-902616-1

Editor: Paul Vanderham
Proofreader: Bernard Shalka
Book Design: Leon Phillips
Cover Design: Gordon Finlay

First printing: 2002

**Creative Connections Publishing**
Suite 212 - 1656 Duranleau • Granville Island
Vancouver, B.C. V6H 3S4 • 604-688-0320 • toll-free 1-877-688-0320
email: ccpublishing@axion.net
**www.creativeconnectionspublishing.com**

*Affiliated Publishers in*
Vancouver • Calgary • Milwaukee • Denver

Printed in Canada

In Memory of Eva,
The Love of My Life

# ACKNOWLEDGEMENTS

Writing this book has made me mindful of and grateful for the persons who have helped me and my wife live out our dreams in Canada: Nanette and Oreste Notte, who took a chance on an unknown young immigrant by giving me a job at the Bon Ton shortly after we arrived in Vancouver; Harry Redl, Gideon Yesudian, Jimmy Chin, and Ernie Bodel, who helped make our Ferguson Point Tea House a success story; Ron Turner, Dave Robertson, Saul Wyne, Lindsay Alexander and Brian Calder, who were true friends and comrades during my real estate years; Elizabeth Holonko (my caregiver), Adele and Earl Moss, Caren and Tom Winkler, and Barbara Whitlock, who stood by me and helped me survive a very difficult period of my life.

The staff at Creative Connections Publishing has guided me through the intricate process of putting this book into print: Paul Vanderham (editor), Leon Phillips (book designer), Gordon Finlay (cover designer), and Jo Blackmore (publisher).

# TABLE OF CONTENTS

# LIST OF ILLUSTRATIONS

# PREFACE

August 28, 1997
Vancouver, B.C.

My Dearest Love,
I could not help noticing a touch of disapproval crossing your face as I read you my first draft of *Escape from Pannonia*. After the reading you were silent for a long time. Later, at dinner, I asked you what you thought of it and whether I had made you unhappy by writing about the events that changed both of our lives. "No," you said, "You did not make me unhappy, but promise me that if you ever publish it you will not do it under your own name." Later, you added, "Anyhow, who is interested in the past, in stories that happened fifty years ago? Maybe you should write about other trips and voyages we did together in the not-so-distant past and under much happier circumstances!"

My dearest, I understand that you would rather forget those terrible years. I, unfortunately, feel differently. I have a deep urge to unburden myself and write about these long-ago, bottled-up events and feelings. I don't want to play the hero. It was not heroism that made me do what I did to escape both the Nazis and the Communists. It was a basic instinct of survival. That same basic instinct urges me to get these memories out of my system somehow; I have to get them down on paper.

Whether *Escape* will ever be published does not matter to me, so for the time being I'll just shelve the whole idea. You should know that I do not want to hurt you. If I have, please forgive me!

Yours forever,
Steve

# INTRODUCTION

It was 5:00 a.m. on a rainy Saturday morning. The misty grey clouds were hanging heavily in the air, covering up the magnificent view of the North Shore mountains, the sea, and the evergreen islands of Howe Sound. While gazing out the window from my study, I muttered to myself, "Look at this lousy, lousy weather. I can't believe it! Is this supposed to be summer? For Christ's sake!"

Then suddenly I stopped cussing. My age-old remedy for chasing away negative thoughts took over. It was so simple. I asked myself, "What if you had stayed in Hungary, never emigrated to Canada? Think man! Where would you be? What would have become of you? You might not even be alive today. And now you are complaining about a little rain and cloud? If you'd stayed in Hungary—and survived to see this day—you'd sure as hell be worrying about a lot more than the weather! You should call yourself lucky, very lucky indeed to be living here in Vancouver."

These thoughts brought with them feelings of deep gratitude for the life that my wife and I had enjoyed here in Canada. They also unleashed a flood of memories of the life I had left behind in Hungary so long ago: Sunday outings with my father, who was fond of showing off his son to his cronies in the beergardens; the smells of foods I have not tasted in many years, including the marvelous spicy aroma of the pub foods mixed with the smell of draught beer and cigarette smoke; the clanging of the streetcar as it rolled down the street; the sight of the Citadel rising above the Danube as it wound through the beautiful heart of Budapest; my first meeting with my future wife, a tiny whisp of a girl sporting a ponytail bound by a red ribbon who smiled at me with her sweet lips and blue eyes; the bittersweet sound of gypsy violins playing Hungarian favorites like "*Csak egy kislany van a vilagon*" ("There Is But One Little Girl in this Whole Wide World") sung to the melody of "Sarasate's Gypsy Airs."

Such pleasant memories filled me with deep feelings of nostalgia for the country of my birth, but they soon gave way to thoughts of the destructive storm clouds of Nazi Germany and the Second World War, which filled me once again with the hopeless sense of being trapped in a giant meat grinder, of being singled out for execution because I was a Jew and therefore, in the eyes of the Nazis and their collaborators, worse than a cockroach. And then came the "liberation" and the Soviet Occupation. What a cruel joke that was. Only the slogans and the catchwords changed: before we had been a menace to the Aryan race; afterwards we became "class-enemies" of the Socialist State.

It was this flood of memories—good and bad, happy and sorrowful—that initially drove me to write this story. All I wanted to do at first was get the memories off my chest. As I wrote, however, I realized that I also wanted to share my story—mine and my wife's—with others. If I didn't do that, I thought, the story would be lost forever. Being childless, my wife and I had never been able to pass it on to another generation. We were the last brittle branch of our family tree, and our story would have died with us. Yet I wanted to pass it on, share with others our escape from the horrors of Nazism and

Stalinism, and, perhaps even more important, I wanted to express our gratitude to Canada for giving us refuge. Now that my wife is gone, killed tragically through my own mistake, I want more than ever to tell our story, which I have kept hidden in my heart for so many years.

On numerous occasions in the course of this story I refer to my Jewish heritage, yet I am not really a religious man at all. You could call me an agnostic. When I was a young man, I considered myself first and foremost not a Jew but a Hungarian. I studied the country's history, loved its literature, its music and its arts. I felt sorry for its great poets and novelists, who were unknown outside the borders of the country merely because they wrote in a language so removed from other living languages that few ever got translated. Bit by bit, however, I became aware that Hungarians were anti-Semitic. My fellow countrymen, I learned, considered Jews to be despicable usurers, exploiters of decent working men, con artists, Christ killers, bolsheviks, capitalists, cheats, seducers of virtuous Christian virgins. The great Hungarian novelist Mikszath Kalman summed up the Hungarian attitude when he described an anti-Semite as a person who despises Jews more than absolutely necessary.

Eventually, this anti-Semitism produced the Holocaust, which I had the good fortune to survive. Compared to those millions who perished in the Nazi extermination camps, my sufferings may seem trivial. Yet to me and the other Hungarian Jews who survived, such suffering was very real, and those of us who did survive have a responsibility to bear witness, especially since there are some who try to deny that the Holocaust ever happened.

**Steve**
with nannies and playmates in front of Parliament Buildings,
Budapest, c. 1924-25

# 1
## GROWING UP
### 1920-1938

I was born in Budapest, Hungary in 1920, two years after the end of World War I, the war that should have ended all wars. The whole country was in turmoil. As punishment for siding with the Germans and Austrians during the war, the victorious Allies had forced Hungary to give up huge chunks of its territory to the newly created countries of Yugoslavia and Czechoslovakia, and also to the old arch-enemy, Romania.

Terrible consequences soon followed. First came a 133-day reign of "Red Terror," a Communist dictatorship established by Hungarian POWs captured on the Russian front during the war and later indoctrinated by Lenin's Bolshevik followers. Next came the reign of the Romanian Army. Supported by the Western Powers, it ended the short-lived Communist dictatorship and occupied the country. After that came the "White Terror" organized by Admiral Horthy and a group of Hungarian officers, who managed to chase out the Romanian troops. Their first agenda was to hang any union organizers or Jews unfortunate enough to fall into their hands from the same lampposts that had recently been used by the "Reds" to hang their "capitalist class enemies." Later their goal would be to align Hungary with Hitler and Mussolini in the hope of regaining the lost territories and realizing the dream of a glorified

"Greater Hungary." Such was the country into which I was born.

My father, who had a college education, was what we would consider upper-middle-class. Prior to the outbreak of the war, he had served as a lieutenant in the Austro-Hungarian Army. He was eventually discharged due to an aggravated stomach ulcer. My mother, his second wife, was twenty-one years his junior. Being a generation apart from each other, they were often engaged in irritating little squabbles. Even so, things went relatively well for them until the Great Depression hit Europe in 1930. Up until then my father had worked as a partner in a prestigious firm on the Budapest Grain Exchange. When the depression hit, he lost his position due to "downsizing." Then all hell broke loose at home, since each of my parents blamed the other for the inevitable lowering of our living standards. Gone were the nannies and the domestic help. Father tried to recover his fortunes by starting a one-man brokerage firm on the Grain Exchange. However, being a proud, scrupulously honest man, he did not thrive financially in the corrupt environment of the day. My mother tried to help out by subletting a bedroom in our house and by opening up a card club. This struggle left its mark on my early years.

My parents tried to make me multilingual. To that end, they chose for me an Austrian nanny. Until the age of six I spoke only German. That was no great advantage when I entered elementary school. Hungarian was the official language, and German-speaking people were frowned upon in the very nationalistic atmosphere of the day. The sweet irony was that our heroic leader Admiral

**Steve**
with mother and father, Budapest,
c. 1924-25

**Grade one class,**
Szemere Street Elementary School,
Budapest, 1926
(Steve second row from back, fourth from right)

Horthy spoke a very poor and heavily accented Hungarian, having spent most of his life in the service of the Austro-Hungarian Navy where both the official and the working language was German.

In elementary school, which was a four-block walk from my home, I learned Hungarian very quickly and at the same time "unlearned" my German. Beyond that I have very little recollection of my elementary school years, except that our teacher for the entire four years was a very kindly old maid called Aunt Sarah.

After elementary school, I attended the Berzsenyi Daniel Gymnasium, which was located in the 5th District of Budapest, a district inhabited largely by the Jewish middle classes. The Hungarians referred to it as "New-Zseland" (Zs from *Zsido*, the Hungarian word for

Jew). The composition of the district was reflected in the make-up of our student body. In my class of sixty-four students, twenty-two were Gentile and forty-two were Jewish. This fact, however, was hardly ever mentioned or taken into consideration by our teachers, who presented the curriculum from a strictly Catholic-Hungarian perspective.

In gymnasium (roughly the European equivalent of Grade 4 to Grade 12) we had to take compulsory classes in Latin and German. I hated both. I considered it a bloody waste of time to learn Latin, a dead language. And I was frustrated by having to master the German Ghotic alphabet, which is quite different from the Latin alphabet used in Romance languages. I also found it difficult to relate the dry grammar to the oral German I had acquired from my Austrian nanny. The German language has three genders: masculine, feminine and neuter, each marked with its respective prepositions: *der, die, das*. And this, my friend, makes German the most cursed grammar in the whole world. It makes no sense to any foreigner how the Germans assign the various genders to their subjects. Girl (*das maedchen*), for example, is neuter in gender, not feminine as you would expect.

However much I disliked studying these languages, I needed them. Hungary, after all, is a small, landlocked country. And unfortunately Hungarian is not related to any other language, living or dead. (I say this in spite of some scholarly opinion that it is related to Finnish and certain Turkic languages of middle Asia.) Nobody five miles beyond the borders of Hungary understands Hungarian. It follows that anyone wanting to leave

9

Hungary, as I did from the time I was a child, needs to learn foreign languages.

It was therefore just as well that in fifth grade of gymnasium we were required to study one more foreign language. We were allowed to choose between ancient Greek and modern Italian. Needless to say, we all chose Italian, a melodic and romantic language, the language of Verdi, Puccini, Rossini, Dante, Petrarch, Boccaccio, Michelangelo, Leonardo da Vinci and Raphael. I should add that we were encouraged to study Italian by our political leaders, who were beginning to cozy up to the fascist dictatorship of Mussolini. In any case, I began to study Italian and discovered, much to my surprise, that the Latin I had learned was actually quite useful in that regard.

Several teachers from the gymnasium stand out in my memory. There was our history teacher, Professor Hlavathy, whose son was a member of our class. To his credit, he never gave any preferential treatment to junior. His attitude, in spite of his Slavic name, was very profoundly Hungarian and patriotic. If he was an anti-Semite, we never found out. He seemed to be totally neutral on the subject. Later on, when Hitler rose to power, he still maintained a very pronounced Hungarian attitude. Historically, this attitude was anti-German, mainly because the German Hapsburgs were the tyrants who had imposed their reign over Hungary for centuries (their initial excuse being their desire to liberate us from the Turks).

Then there was our Latin teacher, Professor Ambrozy, whose nickname was "Thuky." He earned his nickname when, during a long-winded dissertation about the Greek historian Thucydides, he got mixed up completely and for the life of him could not remember the historian's full name. He just kept stammering the first two syllables: "Thuky...Thuky...." Finally he gave up completely. This incident must have happened quite early in his career, but the nickname stuck with him to the end. One result was that he never again digressed from Latin grammar, which we had to recite in parrot-like fashion *ad infinitum*: "ante, apud, ad, versus, circa, citra, cis," etc.

The most memorable teacher of all, however, was Professor Tibor Kardos, who introduced us to Italian. Luckily for us, he differed markedly from all of our other teachers. He was probably the first bohemian intellectual I ever encountered. His method of teaching was modern, even revolutionary. He would show us slides of paintings by the Renaissance masters and sculptures by Michelangelo. He would also organize musical sessions featuring highlights from famous Italian operas, which he would play for us on a hand-winding gramophone.

I was a fairly good student, and my school years would have been quite uneventful if I had not enjoyed playing the role of class clown. But I did enjoy it. Being unable to shine in athletics, I liked being noticed as the "entertainer." By age thirteen I was having huge success imitating the speech and other mannerisms of our teachers. Encouraged by my audience of fellow students, I got bolder and bolder. I was reaching the pinnacle of my success when I discovered the world of telephone pranks. Mine were pretty harmless by today's standards and not very funny. For example, I would dial a number at random and pretend that I was an employee of the telephone company, instructing whoever answered to measure the length of the cord. When they replied with something like, "It is 125 centimeters," I would say, "That is not long enough." They usually asked, "How come?" To which I would say, "It is not long enough for you to hang yourself from the chandelier," and quickly hang up the receiver amidst the howls of my classmates. As I mentioned before, my pranks were not very funny!

My downfall came at age fourteen, when someone else (I was never able to find out who) started to make some very stupid and cruel phone calls, for example, telling the distraught mother of one of my classmates that her son had been killed in a traffic accident. These calls were reported to the principal, who started an investigation. Eventually, I was singled out as the suspected perpetrator. Since the authorities believed that an example had to be made, they came close to expelling me from school. Instead they placed me on probation for one year. They also called in my parents, who promptly grounded me and suspended all my privileges. My father was so angry that he hit me—the only time he ever did so. I was devastated. My one and only goal from then on was to redeem myself! I threw myself into my studies. I devoted myself day and night to obtain good grades and expunge the shame I had brought upon myself and my parents. I really went overboard, denying myself all the little pleasures a boy of my age would naturally have indulged in.

In the process, I lost all my hard-earned popularity with my classmates. They labeled me a "streber." The English equivalent of this word is somewhere between nerd and superachiever, yet the Hungarian word implies teacher's pet. For a boy going through puberty, being burdened with such a name was trying, and I believe it must have left a mark on my sexual development. It did not, however, prevent me from falling in love.

I did this for the first time at age fifteen. Ildiko was tiny and delicate, with beautiful big blue eyes. We met at the ice-skating rink. She was the daughter of the assistant janitor of the apartment building next to where I was living. In the convoluted, snobbish caste system of 1930s Hungary, hers was considered the lowest class imaginable. As a result, I made sure my mother never found out about Ildiko. Ours was an innocent puppy love that never went beyond a few furtive kisses and some awkward fondling. And it did not last long: within six months we had broken up, partly because of the intervention of her parents, who were not too keen on having their daughter getting mixed up with a Jewish boy. No single class in Hungary had a monopoly on prejudice.

Two years after Ildiko it was the Marosi twins. I fell in love with Agi (Agnes). I had no interest at all in her sister Vera, but Vera was hopelessly in love with me. To this day I cannot make sense of this crazy romance, which lasted almost two years, causing me pain, heartache, and sleepless nights, all because Agi completely ignored me. I met her again many years later. At that time she confessed that she had been very much in love with me, but had not wanted to take me away from her twin sister! That meeting really shook me up. Poor Agi had become very fat and ugly, and I could not understand what had attracted me to her so many years before.

At age sixteen, before I became embroiled with the Marosi twins, I had a wonderful surprise that shifted my attention from love to travel. Our Italian teacher, Professor Kardos, had received permission to send two of his students on a six-week holiday in Italy—and one of them was to be me! While in Italy my classmate and I were to be the guests of Il Duce himself: Benito Mussolini. In other words, we were to play our small part in Hungary's plans to forge a friendship with fascist Italy.

These plans, which had emerged in the early 1930s, were motivated by Hungary's awareness of its vulnerability, surrounded as it was by hostile neighbours whose territories had been carved out of the Austro-Hungarian Monarchy: Slovaks, Romanians, Croats, and Serbs—all of whom resented Hungary deeply for helping the Austrians to oppress them under the old regime. Another factor, of course, was the growing power of Hitler's Germany. Hungary's plans to counter these hostile forces explain why, as a boy, I had stood with thousands of other Hungarian schoolchildren waving Italian and Hungarian flags as Italy's King Victor Emmanuel, Admiral Horthy, and Italy's Foreign Minister Count Ciano were driven in ceremonial gilded carriages down the main boulevard of Budapest, escorted by squadrons of Hussars and massive military bands.

The same plans explained why my schoolmates and I were studying Italian, as I've mentioned before. The Hungarian government introduced Italian into the schools, and Il Duce reciprocated by playing host to Hungarian students in Italy. From the point of view of Hungary's plans to align itself with Italy, then, our trip to that country was not all that surprising. What *was*

**Jozsi**
with roadster, Danube Rowing Club,
Budapest, c. 1932

surprising was that Professor Kardos had mustered the courage to select me, a Jewish student, for the privilege of going. The year, after all, was 1936. Hitler had been the chancellor of Germany for three years. The Hungarian Nazi Party, also called the Arrowcross, was getting bolder and louder by the day, and so was the nazi-leaning student fraternity called "Turul" (the name of an extinct, mythical raptor related to the eagle). As a result, of the 200 students selected from Hungarian schools and universities where Italian was taught, only six were Jewish.

To this very day I don't know how I was able to persuade my parents to let me go. They both loved me very much, but they were overly protective. It must have been my

**Jozsi**
skiing in the Swiss Alps,
c. 1935

Uncle Jozsi (Joe), my mother's younger brother, who put the pressure on them. He wanted me to be independent, self reliant, tough, and prepared to leave the country on short notice, if the situation required it. I have always considered Uncle Jozsi a surrogate father and will always be grateful to him. His outlook on life, his ambitions and goals were certainly closer to mine than those of my real father.

Without his guidance and help, I very much doubt that I would have had the stamina to survive the terrible years that were about to darken the skies of Europe. My parents could not give me the hard education I was going to need. They pampered me into becoming a little softy: mama's little darling. Uncle Jozsi had the foresight to toughen me up. He made me tackle sports and athletic activities. He taught me skiing and tennis, and made sure that I joined the school's swimming team. He enrolled me in the Boy Scout movement. He also took me hiking in the Buda mountains and sponsored my application for membership in a prestigious rowing club in Budapest, located on the Danube below the Rose Hill (Rozsadomb) district.

All of Uncle Jozsi's priorities and values were in sharp contrast to my parents' middle-class, Jewish outlook on life. He was an anglophile who tried to lead the life of the British gentry. Right after the end of WWI he converted to.... Well, to be honest I have not the foggiest idea what religion he converted to, since the subject of religion was taboo in his presence. And I certainly never saw him enter a church or a synagogue or found him observing any religious holidays. I do know that he became a broker on the Budapest Futures and Grain Exchange. At age twenty-eight he opened up his own office in partnership with his older brother, my Uncle Miska (Maximillian). Four years later he became the youngest millionaire on the exchange.

During WWI he had served in the Austro-Hungarian Army as a first lieutenant. He was wounded on the Italian Front and later decorated as a hero. Demobilized in 1919, he survived both the Red Terror and the White Terror. It was probably around this time that he decided to break with his Jewish heritage. He changed his family name from Bruck to Bikar and married a German (aryan) woman, my aunt Liesel, the daughter of Admiral Richter, the last German commander of the Kaiser's only East Asian Colony— the Chinese port-city of Tien Tsin (Xinkiang).

But back to my Italian adventure. Before our departure we received our uniforms: black shoes, dark brown socks, brown shorts, yellow shirts and, to top it off, military-style khaki caps. Dressed in these colours, which even today make me want to vomit, we boarded a train at the Southern Railway Station (Deli Palyaudvar) of Budapest and set out for the land of Mussolini. At the Yugoslav border our train was sealed and, as nightfall came, all shades were drawn. This precaution was a sign of the strained relations between Admiral Horthy's Hungary and Yugoslavia. Two years earlier, rumours were circulating that Admiral Horthy was giving financial support and weapons to the right-wing Croatian terrorists who had managed to assassinate Yugoslavia's King Alexander (along with French Foreign Minister Louis Barthou) in Marseilles on October 9th, 1934.

At dawn's first light, our train left the barren, dark Karst Mountains behind. Soon, after a short pause on the Italian border, we sighted the blue Adriatic Sea shimmering 1,000 feet below us in the light of the rising sun. To a sixteen-year-old born and raised in landlocked Hungary, it was an unforgettably beautiful view. From there our train chugged along the Adriatic coast toward Trieste, formerly the principal port of the Austro-Hungarian Empire. As we approached the city, Miramar Castle came into view in all its pink splendour. Built by Emperor Franz Joseph for his beautiful Bavarian-born wife, Empress Elizabeth, it was surrounded by tall cypresses and palm trees, red-tiled roofs, and colourful fishing boats. I was overwhelmed by all this Mediterranean grandeur.

Without stopping, our train passed through Mestre, Bologna, Firenze and the Appenine Mountains. After an uninterrupted eighteen hours on the train, we finally arrived in Rome. There we were quickly transferred to a local train that took thirty minutes to bring us to our final destination, the site of our camp: Ostia, Lido di Roma, which in those days was the Coney Island of Rome.

Our camp was similar to the Boy Scout camps I had attended in my early teens, though the tents were somewhat bigger. We six "Jew-boys" shared one of these tents, where we were often attacked by members of the Nazi-leaning fraternity, Turul. The attacks usually came at night when we couldn't see them coming. I was never harmed myself, but a couple of my friends were beaten up. It would have been futile to report these attacks to the camp commander, who in his younger days had belonged to the same fraternity. Fortunately, we Jewish boys, who spoke better Italian than the other Hungarian students, were able to report the attacks to the local carabinieri (police) guarding the camp and ask them to watch our tent. They were happy to oblige, and the attacks soon stopped.

I should add that, like the carabinieri, the other Italians we met—including the black-shirted fascist youth—seemed to harbour no anti-Semitic feelings. Their lack of prejudice, however, could not protect us completely from the hostility we experienced in our own camp, where we were mistreated and humiliated in numerous ways. During our six-week stay, for example, we were allowed only three furloughs, while the other boys were granted twelve. And we were regularly assigned to the most difficult and least desirable housekeeping duties: garbage detail, kitchen duty, latrine cleaning, etc.

Fortunately, the enjoyments of Rome were only a thirty-minute trainride away and, thanks to our three furloughs, we were able to spend three tremendous days there. We walked in amazement among the ruins of the Roman Forum, where Julius Caesar was knifed by Brutus. And we were awed by the Coliseum, where the gladiators fought to the death. One day I had the thrill of drinking water from a fountain marked SPQR (*Senatus Populusque Romanus*), an inscription that was over two thousand years old. We also visited the ancient Via Appia, Santa Maria Maggiore, Castel San Angelo, and the Vatican, where we saw St. Peter's Basilica, the Sistine Chapel, and the Pieta. At the Trevi Fountain, I dutifully tossed in some coins so that one day I would be able to return to the Eternal City. (And, believe it or not, I did return in 1964. By then, however, Rome was over-run by hordes of tourists.)

On one of our furloughs, we visited the ancient Synagogue of Rome, where we met three members of the congregation. No one would have been able to distin-guish them from the other Italians: they had the same looks, mannerisms, accent, etc. At that time the Jewish population of Rome totaled 30,000 souls. Sephardic in origin, devoutly religious, and loyal followers of Mussolini, they were deeply convinced that Il Duce would protect them from the likes of Hitler. To a certain extent they were right. Only toward the end of the war did Mussolini, who was no anti-Semite, give in to Hitler and allow some Italian Jews to be deported. The majority of Italian Jews were kept in camps in Italy, where they were protected from the Germans—at least until the Germans took over those parts of Italy that were still under their control after the Allied landings and installed a puppet Nazi-Fascist government.

It was in Rome that I ate my first real Italian pasta dish in a little trattoria near the Vatican, which made the food in our camp seem truly atrocious. We got lots of pasta there, to be sure, but it was just barely cooked, sticky, and flavourless (always served without Parmesan cheese). Our real staple, though, was what they called "minestrone." We suspected that the "vegetables" in that soup were picked from the weeds growing in great aban-don all around the camp. Our menu also mentioned *vitello* (veal) and *fegato* (liver), which fuelled rumours that the cats around the camp and even in Ostia proper were mysteriously disappearing at an alarming rate. The poor food in the camp was probably due to the food shortage that followed the League of Nations' decision to impose sanctions against Italy for invading Ethiopia. The tourists were scarce. That shortage coincided with a world-wide depression. Small wonder, then, that in spite of all the posturing and rambling speeches made by Il Duce, the people of Italy had no stomach for either the Ethiopian adventure (or for that matter, the Spanish civil war, where Franco welcomed any troops he could get from his Fascist allies).

Our last furlough to Rome started with a thirty-five minute trainride from the camp in Ostia. We headed for a little trattoria near the Vatican. After devouring a wonderful plate of pasta loaded with ground meat and Bolognese sauce, generously sprinkled with Parmesan cheese, my two friends and I decided to visit the fabulous *Therme di Caracalla* (Baths of Caracalla, made famous again in 1992 when the Three Tenors held their first concert there, under the baton of Zubin Metha).

We had hardly arrived when the heavens opened up and an unexpected thunder shower drenched us completely. We found shelter under the arches and soon discovered that we were not alone. A very fat young man with curly black hair approached us. Greetings were exchanged. When he found out that we were students from Hungary, he offered us his free services as a guide through the ruins. He was friendly and knowledgeable, especially about ancient Roman history. When the rains stopped and we could once again move around to see the sights, we soon discovered that Pietro was an excellent guide. Not until the downpour started up again and we were once again forced to take shelter under the arches did we realize that our guide had ulterior motives. Under the pretext that we had to squeeze close together to avoid getting wet and cold, he put one arm around my friend and with his free hand tried to grab my genitals. Like all good students of Italian, we knew the most obscene Italian cuss words, so we let loose with a barrage and ran to the nearest streetcar stop. It must have been my fastest run ever. This was my first encounter with a homosexual, and it left me quite bewildered and confused.

Towards the end of our stay, our whole group was taken to Naples, where we were allowed to choose between a tour of the city and a trip to the Isle of Capri. A few months earlier I had read Dr. Axel Munthe's book *The Story of San Michele*, which describes the adventures of that great humanitarian Swedish doctor and explains how he built his house in Anacapri. There was no doubt about my choice. I climbed up the steep mountain road leading to Anacapri, where Axel Munthe's magical house, "San Michele," stood overlooking one of the most unforgettable views earth offers. To the east lay the Bay of Naples with the smoke curling up from Mount Vesuvius; to the south was Sorrento and the Amalfi coast. Looking west, you could spot the *Piccola Marina*, the little fishing harbour guarded by those magnificent red rocks called *I Faraglioni*. I had never beheld such beauty. Since the end of the war I have had two more occasions to visit Capri, and although both times I found it overrun by hordes of tourists, for me it has remained the most magical spot in the world.

Before our departure from Italy, our camp received a visit from Il Duce himself. The camp commander arranged to mark the occasion with a great parade. We

**Frau Diamant**
and her international group of students
in Innsbruck.

six Jewish boys, however, were kept carefully out of sight. The authorities gave us a half-day pass to visit the ruins of *Ostia Antica* (Ancient Ostia). There we saw some Roman ruins and a few mosaic floors, and we watched the excavation and restoration work that was in progress. We did not find it very interesting, but were obliged to stay there until Il Duce's visit was over.

Shortly after that visit, our six-week stay came to an end. It was the middle of August, a hot time of the year around Rome. The temperature was hovering near 40 degrees Celsius (90°-100°F). On our return trip, the train stopped in Venice for eight hours, leaving us time for an unforgettable tour of the sights: the Piazza San Marco, the Doge Palace, St. Marks Basilica, the Campanile, and the Rialto Bridge. We would have dearly loved to take a gondola ride, or even a commuter-boat ride, on the Grand Canal. But our leaders locked us up in a schoolyard for the final three hours of our brief stay. Then, when our train was ready to roll again, they released us. To this day my trip to Italy is deeply etched in my memory: the sights, sounds, and smells of the railway stations; the fresh-perked espresso served at sidewalk cafés; the Parmesan cheese melting over hot pasta; the masterpieces of Leonardo da Vinci, Michelangelo, Raphael, Bellini; the ringing of church bells; the sweet, sad sounds of the Neapolitan songs performed by street musicians and singers; the cries of news vendors; and the melody of the hit song of the day: *Facetta nera, d'Abyssinia:* "Little black face of Ethiopia, don't be afraid of us, as we will bring you another Duce and another King!"

In the summer of 1937, thanks to Uncle Jozsi who paid for it all, I attended an exclusive, private summer-camp in Tyrol, Austria, which was run by a Jewish lady from Vienna. The students who gathered there under Frau Diamant's firm but benevolent leadership were a cosmopolitan mixture of young Jewish students from Hungary, Czechoslovakia, Yugoslavia, Austria, and France. We met our denmother in Vienna and then travelled by train through the beautiful Austrian countryside to the province of Tyrol. Our camp was approximately twenty miles east of Innsbruck in the magnificent valley of the Inn River. I remember that the nearest railway station was in Jenbach or Brixlegg, depending on whether you took the local train or the Orient Express. Our "camp" was one of those gorgeous tyrolean farmhouses with a gabled roof and huge flower boxes overladen with white and red geraniums. In the barn, big brown cows supplied us with milk. Not far away, a path wound along beside a swift-running creek that drove an old wooden waterwheel on its way to a charming alpine lake by the name of Achensee. Weather permitting, we swam there every day.

My best friends among my "fellow inmates" were from Prague and Bratislava. They opened my eyes to some of the prejudices of my upbringing. As part of my education in Hungary, I was taught to hate all people coming from our neighbouring countries. Yet my new friends and I got along famously. The younger son of Frau Diamant, Bobby, a very charming and highly intelligent youngster, was also a member of our group. So were three or four Viennese girls, who were vigilantly chaperoned by our denmother. Much of this vigilance was unnecessary, since the girls were without exception very homely. Lucky for us, though, they all had a great sense of humour and thus were excellent company. The food was simple but delicious. All in all we had a happy, carefree time.

We swam, played games, told stories and jokes, and went to the village cinema at least once a week. On rainy days Frau Diamant took us to a charming little medieval town called Rattenberg, which was squeezed in between the fast flowing Inn River and the alpine foothills. The town's most attractive feature was perhaps its *konditorei* (pastryshop), where we gorged ourselves often on wonderful Austrian delicacies: *Indianer Krapfen, Bezets, Topfen Taschkerl, Dobosch Torten* and, of course, the Austrian staple: *Schlagobers* (whipped cream, for all you uninitiated).

To quote Dickens, "It was the best of times," to be sure, and it was also "the worst of times." In August of 1937, the infamous *Anschluss* (Annexation) was only eight months away. The Nazi propaganda machine was already in full swing. Austria's Chancellor Kurt von Schuschnigg, the successor to the murdered Dolfuss, was a mild-mannered bureaucrat, certainly no match for Hitler. And Schuschnigg had recently lost his only potential saviour, Benito Mussolini, who owed Hitler for his supporting Italy's adventures in Ethiopia and Albania. The Italians, furthermore, were also fighting side by side with German soldiers in the Spanish civil war: thus, they would not lift a finger to prevent Hitler's annexation of Austria.

When I look back on that summer of 1937, I think we must have been totally blind and living in a fool's paradise. The handwriting was literally on the walls: the granite faces of the awesomely beautiful Austrian Alps were covered with Nazi propaganda and graffiti. Swastikas, hate slogans against Jews, and the dreaded word *Anschluss* were everywhere. And little Tyrolean schoolchildren could be heard marching and singing the Horst Wessel song promising that Jewish blood would spurt to the skies. This ugly reality started to hit home when we made an excursion to nearby Kufstein, an infamous fortress-prison on the German border, where the Habsburgs used to imprison all the rebels who tried to throw off the Austrian yoke. Kufstein was disturbing in itself: in its dungeons we could read the pained messages scrawled on the walls by tortured and shackled political prisoners, many of whom were Hungarian patriots, including the heroes of the failed 1848 uprising against Austrian rule. But what really terrified us was that, although Kufstein was in Austrian territory, there were no Austrian flags to be seen anywhere. The swastika, by contrast, was flying everywhere. And the local youths, almost without exception, were dressed in the uniform of the Hitler Youth.

Many times over the years I have wondered what fate befell the friends I made in Austria: the Diamant family, the Czech and Slovak boys whose names I have forgotten, and the Parisian girl whose name was Madelaine Cerf. Did any one of them survive the Holocaust? I never ever heard anything from or about them after that summer of 1937.

At that time we had no real understanding of the cataclysm that was about to shatter the peace of Europe and destroy the lives of millions. But when we returned to school in Hungary in the fall of 1937, we did so with misgivings about what the future would hold for the class of 1938. Those misgivings would soon prove to be justified. Some seven months later, on March 12, 1938, our history teacher, Professor Hlavathy, interrupted his class to make a somber announcement: Austria, our neighbour to the west, had ceased to exist. The *Anschluss* was accomplished without a single shot being fired. When Hitler marched into Vienna on March 13th, the movie newsreels showed a jubilant crowd showering the troops with rose petals. The pretext for the annexation was the plebiscite that Chancellor Schuschnigg had intended to hold on the question of union with Germany. The Germans cancelled that plebiscite immediately, then a few days later, held one of their own in the shadow of the Nazi tanks. They got the vote they wanted: 99.6% of Austrians eligible to vote were in favour of annexation. This result may be attributed in part to the presence of the German army, in part to

German propaganda. But it also expressed the prevailing public sentiment, as I knew from my visit to Austria in 1937.

March 15th—the Ides of March—is one of the great patriotic holidays of Hungary, marking as it does the anniversary of the 1848 uprising against Habsburg rule. The great Hungarian poet, Alexander Petofi, recited his famous, rousing poem on that occasion, while standing on the steps of Pest[1] City Hall: "Rise Hungarians, the Fatherland calls on you, Swear to the God of Hungary, that we shall be slaves no more." Ninety years later, on March 15, 1938, Nazi Germany had become our neighbour to the west. There were a few cheers, mostly from the ranks of the ever bolder Arrowcross (the Hungarian Nazi Party) and from among the ethnic Germans (*Volks-Deutsche*) living amongst us. But most Hungarians were anxious. As for Admiral Horthy, he too must have felt apprehensive. Yet the possibility of recovering lost territory from Czechoslovakia and therefore fulfilling the dream of a "Greater Hungary" must have blinded him, for he soon declared his loyalty to Hitler.

---

1. The City of Budapest came into being when the three municipalities: Buda, Pest and Obuda were amalgamated towards the end of the nineteenth century.

Andy Szivo,
1940

# 2

## THE WAR YEARS
## 1939-1945

In 1938 I graduated with honours. But so what? A few months after my graduation, the first "Jewish laws" were proclaimed. For Jews, no higher education was possible any longer. We were excluded from all the professions and all white-collar jobs. All Jewish businesses were supposed to be racially cleansed or "aryanized": both euphemisms for expropriation. Some businesses were allowed to retain their former Jewish bosses as employees, but only until the "Aryans" received sufficient training in the intricacies of the business. After that even the former bosses could be dismissed. Yes, there were loopholes in the beginning. Many Jewish businessmen managed to become journeymen and even foremen in their own businesses.

As graduates of the class of 1938, we skipped the idea of a university education and concentrated on landing an apprenticeship in one of the various trades. We thought such an apprenticeship would serve us well if we ever managed to emigrate to a foreign country. "Tradesmen are always in demand the world over!" This statement became the cliché of Jewish parents throughout Central Europe, just as the phrase "My son the Doctor" became a cliché for Jewish parents in North America. Nobody really had any idea how this pursuit of a trade would work out, and no one, especially not my parents, had the slightest inclination to let their precious son emigrate. Nonetheless, we tried our best to pursue a trade of one kind or another.

I was fortunate. My uncle Emery (Imre), my father's youngest brother, was a one-third partner in a prestigious pastryshop-cum-chocolate-and-candy-factory. Their business had already been racially cleansed, and they needed someone reliable to handle the books and control the mostly gentile employees. So my uncle hired me as an apprentice. It soon became quite clear to me that my "apprenticeship" was a convenient excuse for my bosses to have a very cheap junior executive who had nowhere to go to complain about being exploited. I worked an average of seventy-two hours a week and was paid the minimum wage with no extra earnings for overtime.

Fortunately for me, however, my employers were obliged to keep up appearances to satisfy the inspectors watching over former Jewish businesses. Thus, I was able to spend at least some time in the bakery. Combined with the compulsory classes for apprentices at trade school, this allowed me to learn the basics. After three years of apprenticeship, I even managed to "graduate" and obtain a journeyman's certificate.

These were dark days. A heavy cloud of hopelessness hung over us. There was no physical suffering, I had my three square meals every day and I had shelter, still living as I was with my parents. Yet a long series of daily humiliations was inflicted on us by the ever-tightening grip of the "Jewish Laws." In accordance with these laws, all Jewish professionals were expelled from their respective associations and restricted to serving only other Jews. The same went for actors, writers, producer, etc.

My uncle's junior partner, Joe Steiner, hired an apprentice of his own. I guess it was an attempt by him to counterbalance my presence in the factory and have someone to monitor my activities on his behalf. His name was Andrew Szivo. Two years older than I, his overriding ambition in life was to deflower as many girls as he was physically able to. Neither the work at the factory, the apprenticeship nor any other pursuit was of much interest to him, although he did enjoy playing bridge and the violin. He was handsome and charming and, at the time we met, deeply in love with a young Austrian nanny. Under the racial laws in effect in Hitler's 1000-year Reich (which at that time included Austria), any intercourse between an Aryan woman and a Jewish man (called *rassenschande* or racial shaming) was punishable by the death of the male lover. Hungary had enacted similar laws; however, at that time the maximum penalty was only imprisonment or deportation to a labour camp.

One day Andy did not show up for work. No one, including his sponsor, Joe Steiner, or his immediate family knew of his whereabouts. Two weeks later a very tired Andy showed up again wearing a big, happy smirk on his face. It turned out that he had paid a visit to his girlfriend who at that time was living with her family in the Styrian Alps. The two of them, according to Andy, had retreated to a small mountain cabin (also owned by her family) and made love for a solid two weeks, hardly ever stopping for food or drinks. It was hard to believe that the woman's brother, a member of the dreaded SS who was searching for the two lovers with a loaded shotgun, did not manage to find them.

Steve,
1942

**Eva,**
1942

After the war this story was confirmed by the woman herself.

Andy was lucky that time, but his good fortune could not last. In the summer of 1941 Hitler started an undeclared war with the Soviet Union. Hungary was forced to send troops. Andy was drafted into a labour battalion where Jews were doing the required military service. His battalion was among the first transports sent out to the Russian Front. A short while later it was captured by the Red Army, who did not bother to distinguish between the Fascist troops and their Jewish slaves. All were sent to the Gulags in Siberia. For the next six long years, I did not hear a word from Andy.

I missed him very much for we had become fast friends during our apprenticeship. Without him around, I had little to do after hours, so I buried myself in my work. In the summer of 1942, however, an old school chum of mine named Leslie asked me to join him for a double blind-date. He told me that the woman he was dating, Manyi, would be accompanied by Eva, her cousin. Being tired of Manyi, Leslie wanted to swap her for Eva. My role was to take Manyi off his hands.

Our outing took place on August 20th, when Hungarians celebrate the coronation of their patron saint, namely St. Stephen, the king who converted the pagan Magyar tribes to Christianity. Traditionally the occasion is marked by fireworks and processions in which the holy relics of St. Stephen (including his mummified right hand) are paraded through the city in a bejewelled glass case. Whole oxen are barbecued, and all the young folks put on their best finery. This is usually a day of joyous celebration, but 1942 was a sad exception to the rule, for on that day the German Luftwaffe, on direct orders from Hitler, shot down the plane of Admiral Horthy's son, a captain in the Hungarian Air Force. The incident was of course blamed on the Russians. Young Horthy was murdered because he was openly pro-western and because during the early war years he had maintained sympathies and connections with the Allies. The day of his death was declared a National Day of Mourning. The city was bedecked with black flags. The radio played funeral dirges all day.

Amidst this official sadness, Leslie and I headed to the old town of Buda for our double blind-date. The grey stucco apartment house at Marvany Street was typical of the turn-of-the-century buildings situated in the old town: nondescript and unpromising.

As soon as we arrived we heard giggling. It was obvious that the women had kept a lookout for us. Leslie went inside on his own, while I waited at the door. Ten minutes later he emerged with Manyi and her cousin Eva. Unfortunately for Leslie, all the pre-arranged signals and agreements were forgotten. Eva smiled at me, put her arms in my arms, and we walked ahead. Leslie and Manyi ambled after us unhappily. Eva was tiny, her big eyes full of mischief, her perfect figure crowned by a lovely oval face. She was so happy amidst all the the official gloom and doom. As corny as it may sound, it was love at first sight for both of us. Bubbling with joy, she sang and danced along the dark streets. If I had not fallen so totally in love with her, I might have been a bit embarrassed by her exuberance.

We went to St. Margaret's Island, a lovely little park in the middle of the Danube. The establishment we visited was called the Casino, but it had nothing to do with gambling. While in the afternoon housewives gathered there to gossip over coffee and tea, in the evening it was a romantic place for young lovers. That evening a trio was playing the latest hits from America, translated into Hungarian and thus disguised from the ever-so-watchful eyes of the censors. That first date with Eva changed my life forever. Yes, she changed it. As it turned out we both felt from the first moment that we had known each other for many long years.

Her story was quite remarkable. She came from a musical family. Her grandfather was a famous operatic tenor at the turn of the century. He raised his son Willy, Eva's father, to become a conductor. Eva's mother, Julia, had become a concert singer under her husband's tutelage. Eva herself, not surprisingly, was endowed with a golden voice, though she never admitted it, claiming that she was barely in league with her mother. She had been born in Budapest in 1920. A few weeks after the blessed event, her mother left her in care of her grandparents and joined Willy her husband in Berlin, where he was pursuing a promising career as an opera conductor.

The two must have been engrossed by the flourishing culture of that city, since it took them five years to remember the daughter they had left behind in Hungary. Having finally sent for her, they met her at Berlin's Grand Central Station. Eva was anxious to meet her long-lost parents. As the train pulled into the station, she pressed her nose tight against the window. That might have somewhat distorted her lovely little face. In any case, Willy took one look at her, then buried his face in

St. Margaret's Island,
site of our first date

Map of Central **Budapest**

**Eva's parents,**
Julie and Willy Schmidt, c. 1969

his hands and ran away, shouting, "Oh for heaven's sake, what an ugly duckling!" So it was only Julia who took the little girl home by cab.

Eva's life with her parents, already fragile, would not survive Hitler's rise to power. Under the Nuremberg racial laws, Willy was only half Aryan (or half Jewish); Julia, a Lutheran convert, was 100% Jewish. Eva had been raised as a Lutheran and did not have the faintest idea that under German law she was considered 75% Jewish. She hardly thought of herself as Jewish at all until, at the age of fourteen, she was called up to the blackboard by a teacher who wanted to show the class what Semitic racial features look like. By that time, Willy's Jewishness had made it impossible for him to find employment in Berlin. He was therefore touring the provinces with a cast of second- and third-rate actors and singers making many one-night stands. This hardship seems to have pushed the family to the breaking point.

The break itself happened in a small town in Saxony, near the Czech border, where Eva was studying for her confirmation with a sympathetic minister who had taken her under his wing in spite of her racial origins. The year was 1934. One morning Eva woke up to find her parents gone and herself abandoned in an unfamiliar town and surrounded by bigoted, hostile strangers. The local innkeeper, with whom the parents had stayed before vanishing, took her in and put her to work. In exchange for fourteen hours of back-breaking work, she got scraps of food and shelter in an unheated barn. After racking her brains for a way to contact her Hungarian relatives, she somehow managed to send a letter to her uncle Marczi

(Martin), who worked for the Hungarian State Railway Company.

Thanks to his railway connections, Uncle Marczi was able to arrange for her to cross the Czech border, traverse the country, and re-enter Hungary. There, he and his wife Anna welcomed Eva into their home, a modest one-bedroom apartment which they occupied with their four children. The four cousins were all older than Eva. Leslie, the oldest boy, and his brother Bandi, two years younger, were working as clerks. The two girls, Manyi and Edith, had no jobs. The apartment was crowded and the family budget was limited, but Anna and Martin were pleased to welcome their young niece. To her dying day, Eva regarded them as her true parents, and their children as her brothers and sisters. At the time, however, she knew that they could ill afford to give her room and board in the long run. So she resolved to either contribute to the family coffers or strike out on her own.

She first got a job as a German language teacher. Later, after another uncle (the black sheep of the family) discovered that she had a beautiful voice, she began a career as a nightclub singer. That engagement would nearly be Eva's death, mainly because of German military intervention in the Balkans. By 1941 Hitler's *Wermacht* had already conquered Poland and overrun the Low Countries and France. And Rommel's panzer divisions were bolstering Italy's North African defences. In order to protect the southern underbelly of Europe, Hitler ordered his troops to subdue Yugolslavia and Greece. He also ordered Hungary to send troops to these Balkan countries in support of the *Wermacht*.

For Hungary's prime minister, Count Teleky, this was a disastrous turn of events. Hungary was, of course, a willing Axis partner by this time. But Teleky had just concluded a non-aggression pact with Yugoslavia, guided by German diplomatic efforts to coax the Yugolsalvs into joining the Axis Powers. The sudden shift from diplomacy to a ruthless military campaign constituted, for Teleky, a terrible betrayal and an unbearable loss of honour. The day he heard the news, he put a gun to his temple and blew his brains out.

For Admiral Horthy, however, the German invasion of the Balkans presented Hungary with an opportunity to recapture territories it had lost after World War I. Those territories included two regions in Yugoslavia that contained some of the best farmland in Europe. Called Banat and Bacska, they were famous for high-yielding crops and fast-gaining livestock. The largest city of the regions was Novi Sad, which had a mixed population of Hungarians, Germans, Gypies and Jews. Once Hitler returned control of Banat and Bacska to Hungary, Admiral Horthy sent in the dreaded gendarmes, a Hungarian paramilitary force noted for its rooster-feathered caps and its ruthless brutality. Their mission was to "keep order."

The Hungarian force arrived in Novi Sad just before Christmas. Eva had arrived earlier in the day. Tired after a long rail journey, she had gone to bed early. At 4:00 a.m. a troop of gendarmes burst into the hotel. Everyone was ordered out. There was no time to get dressed. Eva managed to put a winter coat over her nightie and slip into her high-heeled evening shoes. There was no time to look for her snowboots. The temperature was hovering in the minus ten degree Celsius range. The gendarmes were yelling and beating all stragglers with their rifle butts. The hotel guests were marched down to the Danube, which was frozen solid. They were lined up in groups of twenty to thirty and made to stand on the ice in the freezing darkness. As the orders came in from headquarters, the shivering hostages were taken in groups to the edge of the open water and mowed down with machineguns. Who was caught in this mini-holocaust? All the Jews, Gypsies, Serbs and transients who had been driven out of the hotels and boarding houses: men and women, young and old— anyone whose face was not to the gendarmes' liking. Some estimate that anywhere from 4,000 to 20,000 hostages were massacred that night. The censored Hungarian press reported only minor skirmishes between Cetnik guerrillas and the army. Only after the war did people learn the gruesome truth about what took place on that winter night in Novi Sad.

Eva stood with her group for hours. After dawn, a young lieutenant, seeing Eva shivering in her high-heeled evening shoes and thin winter coat, took pity on her. He yelled over to her, "Follow me!" She soon found herself in a railroad marshalling yard where a train loaded with Hungarian refugees was about to pull out. He shoved her on. Eva locked herself in the washroom. Twelve hours later the train rolled into Budapest's South Railway Station.

This all happened eight months before we met. Due to heavy censorship of the media, I was totally unaware of the massacre at Novi Sad until I met one of my rowing mates from the Duna Club (which incidentally was expropriated by the end of 1941). We met on the street, and I noticed something very strange. At a previous meeting a few weeks earlier he had had wavy black hair, but now it was snow white. When I asked him what happened, he told me that he had been taken hostage in Novi Sad that night in December, 1941. He said he would never forget it. Neither would Eva.

Having made it back to Budapest, Eva sought refuge with her parents. Since their escape from Germany in 1937, they had been living in a northern suburb of Budapest, where they managed to eke out a modest living by teaching piano and giving singing lessons. When Eva showed up at the doorstep of their small rented bungalow, hungry and shivering with fever, the reception she got from Willy was as icy as the Danube at Novi Sad. She started telling him about her incredible escape from the hell she had been through. He asked, "Where is your luggage, your clothes, your ration card?" Her answer—that she had been lucky to escape with her life and the winter coat on her back—did not satisfy him. He called her a liar and a whore, and chased her out of the house. Her mother, always more compassionate, hid her in the unheated garden shed for the night and brought her a bowl of warm soup.

The next morning Eva set out on foot to see Aunt Anna and Uncle Martin. The snow was knee high. It took her many hours slogging to reach the apartment on Marvany Street. Once there, she promptly collapsed. It was soon discovered that she had pneumonia. Fortunately for her, Eva's surrogate family gave her the help she needed, as they had done before. Within a matter of weeks they nursed her back to health. It was shortly after, in the summer of 1942, that we met.

As I mentioned before, we were soon deeply in love. Within several days I was thinking seriously of spending the rest of my life with Eva. Of course our shaky present and uncertain future did not bode well for marriage and long term commitments. But we were determined. I therefore introduced her to my family, which turned out to be a big mistake. Not only did both of my parents reject Eva, but to my great disappointment, so did my enlightened Uncle Jozsi. We did not fare any better with her parents. Willy was distressed that his only daughter, who was raised as a Lutheran was falling for a Jew, thus bringing the family back full circle to its roots. As far as my family was concerned, they felt I could do much better than tie the knot with a penniless nightclub singer.

Willy was so determined to destroy our relationship that he forced a "fiancé" on Eva. Cornel was of Aryan stock and was involved in shady black market activities. This made him flush with money, unlike me. Willy totally accepted and approved of him. When Cornel learned about our affair, he became very jealous. I never met him, but Eva warned me that he could be very dangerous and that I should watch out. As it happened, that warning was well founded.

In May of 1943, a warrant was issued for my arrest. I was called in to Police Headquarters, where a sergeant began interrogating me. I was told that a few days earlier I had been overheard making loud, derogatory remarks about Horthy and the current regime in an upscale restaurant frequented by the local Nazi establishment. Eva and I both suspected Cornel as the source of this accusation.The charge was preposterous. For many years no liberal-minded Hungarians or Jews would go near the "Mathias Cellar" unless they were obsessed with suicidal wishes. Even the sergeant interrogating me did not quite believe the charge, so he gave me a face-saving alternative to a lengthy jail sentence. I could "voluntarily" join a labour battalion within one week and my record would be wiped clean.

The month of May can be the most beautiful time of the year in Budapest. The nights are balmy, the lilacs bloom, and their fragrance fills the air. On such a night, before I had to report to the barracks to join my labour battalion, Eva and I had dinner in a little garden restaurant. We drank wine and listened to a three-piece Gypsy band playing our favourite songs. Both of us got a little tipsy. Part way through the evening Eva began to sing some of those sad Hungarian Gypsy songs. Every note came from the heart. At 2:00 a.m. the headwaiter asked us to leave since the restaurant was closing. Without missing a beat or saying anything, Eva picked up one of the pressurized soda bottles the waiters had served with the wine, took perfect aim at the big bass, and sprayed the contents into the artistically curved ribs without one drop going astray. A generous tip to the musicians saved me from an embarrassing incident.

Eight hours later I was marching in tight formation with other members of my labour battalion to Budapest's South Railway Station. A tiny wisp of a woman in a bright flowing skirt followed our group. Her hair was tied in a pony-tail and her gorgeous blue eyes were filled with tears. Before the train pulled out, we managed one last embrace.

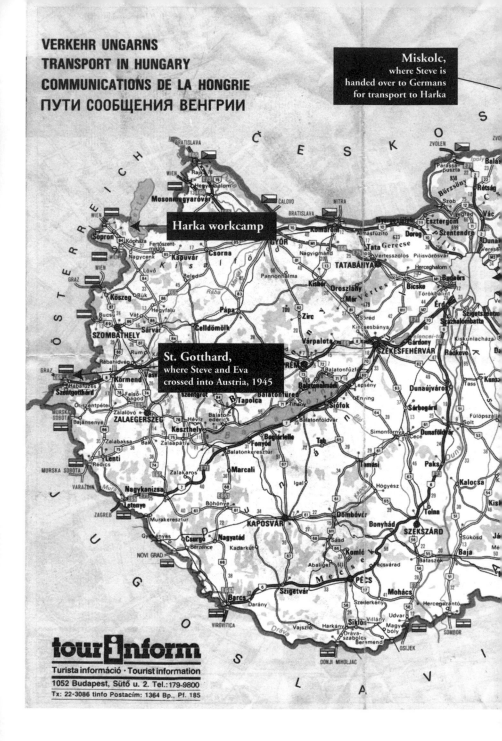

# VERKEHR UNGARNS
# TRANSPORT IN HUNGARY
# COMMUNICATIONS DE LA HONGRIE
# ПУТИ СООБЩЕНИЯ ВЕНГРИИ

**Miskolc,**
where Steve is
handed over to Germans
for transport to Harka

**Harka workcamp**

**St. Gotthard,**
where Steve and Eva
crossed into Austria, 1945

**tour info rm**
Turista információ · Tourist information
1052 Budapest, Sütő u. 2. Tel.:179-9800
Tx: 22-3086 tinfo Postacím: 1364 Bp., Pf. 185

48

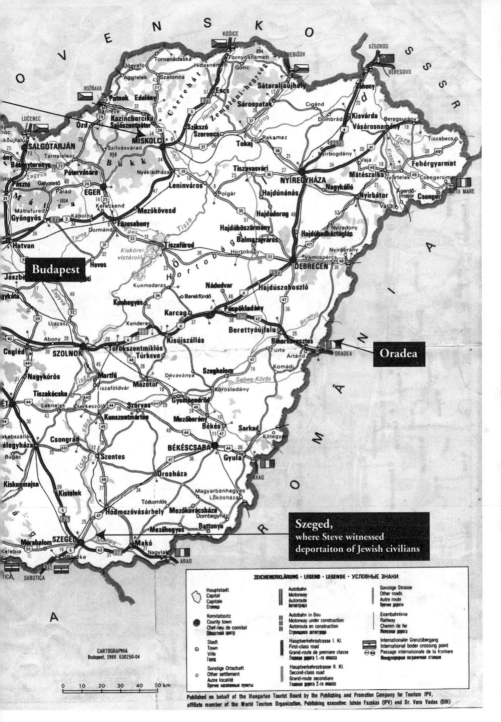

Map of **Hungary**

The labour battalion's first assignment brought us to the newly "liberated" south, which had formerly belonged to Yugoslavia: the great farming country of Bacska. After three days of digging foxholes and tank traps, I was transferred to the kitchen. Our commandant had found out about my apprenticeship in my uncle's factory and decided to put me to work as a cook. I guess this lucky break—and the apprenticeship that made it possible—saved my life during the next two years of service in the labour battalions. Even so, the work in the kitchen was not easy, and it certainly carried responsibilities and hazards. Cooks had to get up two hours before the troops and they usually did not finish cleaning up until one hour after the troops retired. It was a fourteen- to sixteen-hour workday seven days a week. But the benefits of the work outweighed all the hardships. For the next one-and-a-half years I was never hungry or cold and, due to my enviable position, I had lots of friends—fellow inmates, guards and officers alike.

After two months in Bacska, we were sent to a godforsaken little village near the town of Oradea Mare in territories ceded to Hungary by Romania. I was feeling millions of miles away from Eva when one day, to my amazement, she arrived to pay me a visit. A sympathetic sergeant of the guards managed to give me a two-day furlough. Eva and I went to Oradea Mare and, after taking a bath, we spent the next two days making love in a little residential hotel.

The summer of 1944 was the beginning of the end for most Hungarian Jews living outside of Budapest. A new military government, established in March of that year, systematically rounded up all Jews except those already serving in the labour battalions. This was the start of the deportations of women, children and old people to Poland's extermination camps: Auschwitz, Treblinka and Sobibor. We had no idea what was going on. One morning in June of 1944, our battalion was moved again, this time to the Russian front. Along the way our train stopped in the second largest city of Hungary: Szeged, famous for its authentic paprika. We saw thousands upon thousands of women, children and old folks—all wearing the yellow Star of David—lugging their meager belongings as they were loaded into cattle cars by the gendarmes. They told us that they were on their way to Germany to work in the war industries. They believed it and we believed it. It was only after the war ended that we learned of their real fate.

From Szeged our train chugged its way to the Carpathian mountains, then passed into a region that used to be Poland. Not far from the once famous Polish ski resort of Mykuliczyn, our train stopped and we bunked down in open fields near the little village of Szvety Stephan. All through the night we heard artillery bombardment and machine gun fire. Early in the morning, after I had served breakfast to the troops, a messenger came and I was ordered to leave everything behind and accompany him to Headquarters. I was nervous, since cooks were targeted for periodical audits of the supplies and rations. Because the guards had access to everything and frequently helped themselves to whatever they could steal, no one had an absolutely clean slate. But the cooks, whether guilty or innocent, were usually blamed. So I entered Headquarters expecting the worst.

I was led into an elegant room in the confiscated castle of an escaped Polish count. The elderly captain looked up from his paperwork and greeted me with a friendly, "Good morning, Son! Tell me, is it true that you have been working as a journeyman at the Floris Pastryshop?" "Yessir," was my answer. So he told me that he needed a good, qualified cook for his officer's mess. I was soon cooking for thirty-two persons. I had one helper, a Jewish butcher by the name of Joe Schwartz, who cooked the soups and prepared the meat dishes. My task was to compose the menus, make sauces, cook vegetables and bake pastries for dessert. Together we made elaborate breakfasts, three-course luncheons, and suppers and midnight snacks every day.

I could not believe my good fortune, especially after I heard that my whole battalion had been caught by the advancing Russians one day after I was transferred. Most were killed on the spot; the rest wound up in Siberian Gulags, as I learned later from one of my surviving comrades. To the best of my knowledge there were only five survivors among the 250 men captured by the Russians, who did not differentiate between the German soldiers and their Jewish slave labourers.

Shortly after joining the HQ staff, I received a short censored note from my mother informing me that my father had passed away on June 6th. He was seventy-two years old. He had died of bleeding stomach ulcers. In prior years, with good medical care, he easily survived these periodic attacks. But this was 1944. When his ulcers acted up this time, he was brought in a wheelbarrel to a school auditorium serving as a "Jewish Hospital" and left there to die without anyone looking after him. My mother told me later that his last words expressed his desire to say goodbye to me. Poor dad! Yet in a way his death was fortunate, for he was spared the events that followed, events that would soon put an end to the relative safety I enjoyed in my position at HQ.

As long as Captain Bardossy was in charge there, we Jews (myself, Joe Schwartz, and Bardossy's driver, Peter Kertesz) were treated fairly. We wore the regular uniforms of the Hungarian infantry, and we were not required to display the hated yellow armband with the Star of David. Anyone who abused us verbally or assaulted us physically was severely reprimanded by the captain. Unfortunately for us, however, the captain was recalled to Budapest early in October 1944. His second in command, Lieutenant Sandor Gergely, took over.

After the war I had occasion to meet with Captain Bardossy. I visited him in the army barracks and learned that under the new regime, he was able to retain his rank. I thanked him for saving my life and offered him my testimony or any other help he might need to prove that he was not in league with the Nazi officers who were in charge of the Jewish labour battalions. He politely declined.

I never did learn exactly why Bardossy had been transferred. Perhaps it was related to the increased intensity of the Russian offensive. Shortly before the transfer, the Red Army had reconquered the Ukraine, broken through the German and Hungarian defenses in the Carpathian Mountains, and pushed into Hungary. As the Russians advanced, we and the

Hungarian Army retreated deeper and deeper into Hungary.

On October 15, 1944, soon after Bardossy's departure, Admiral Horthy suddenly realized that he had made a bad bargain by joining the Axis, so he quickly offered the Allies unconditional surrender and expressed his willingness to sign a separate peace treaty with them. These moves, however, were too little and too late. The Germans promptly captured Horthy and incarcerated him in Austria. They then installed a puppet Nazi regime in Hungary, namely the Arrowcross, which was headed by an Armenian fanatic by the name of Ferenc Szalasi.

He initiated a true reign of terror featuring mass deportations and indiscriminate killings of Jews and Gypsies. As usual, we soldiers in the field knew next to nothing of what was going on. But Lieutenant Gergely, who always resented the "privileged" treatment we had received from Captain Bardossy, undoubtedly knew which way the wind was blowing. One October morning he had us three Jews arrested and delivered to the Arrowcross in the town of Miskolc in northern Hungary. We were stripped of our uniforms and herded into waiting cattle cars.

The transport from northern Hungary to the Austrian border took three long days. We received the standard treatment for Jews headed for the concentration camps: eighty to one hundred of us were crammed into a car reeking of urine and excrement. We were given no food or water. We had no space to rest or lie down. The guards beat us mercilessly. Many died, but they were not removed until we arrived in the little border village of Harka.

Located at the western edge of Hungary near the Austrian province of Burgenland, Harka was then being transformed into a giant work camp where thousands of slave-labourers were forced to build tank traps, foxholes and other fortifications designed to halt the Russian advance toward Vienna. For the next six months I would be one of the inmates.

As strange as it may seem to say so here, my apprenticeship at my uncle's factory had served me well indeed. It had not worked out as we originally hoped it would, yet it had left me strong enough to survive the journey to Harka. When I arrived, I was in relatively good physical condition, and I would need every ounce of strength in order to survive the ordeal that lay ahead.

**Jewish Labour Battalion**
in Southern Hungary, 1943
(Steve, first row standing fifth from left)

# 3

## ESCAPE FROM THE NAZIS

The conditions in the camp at Harka were not unlike those in the dreaded concentration camps: the only features missing were the gas chambers and the ovens. We suffered from a starvation diet, unheated barracks, frequent beatings, and severe punishments for the slightest breach of the rules. And we fell ill from typhoid, dysentery, etc.

The absence of gas chambers, crematoria ovens or striped uniforms can easily be explained. The German High Command as well as the SS in charge of deportations and the camps did not expect to fight the Russians so close to the border of the Third Reich. So when the fortunes of the war suddenly shifted in favour of the Allies, they had to improvise and set up fortifications in a hurry, leaving no time for the elaborate extermination systems to be implemented. Besides, they needed every able-bodied human to build tank traps and foxholes.

I can credit this situation for an SS guard saving my life. One cold November morning when we reported for the customary roll call, they did not march us to work. A high-ranking SS officer, who had come along with our regular older guards, made a speech. He told us that those who did not feel fit enough to do the heavy work should step forward, so that they could be transported to a factory where the indoor work would be much easier. He emphasized that only those in very poor condition should step forward. In those days I was still in relatively good health, yet ignorant as to the real meaning of this unbelievably kind gesture coming from a SS colonel. But the offer of having it easier blinded me, so I stepped forward.

The guard who was watching over me at work immediately jumped forward and started beating me with his rifle-butt. "Go back, you son of a bitch, lazy stinking Jew!" he yelled. "Didn't you hear what the Colonel just said! Back to digging foxholes and don't you forget it!" To drive home his point, he beat my face until the blood ran. I lost six teeth but escaped the last transport to an extermination camp.

Work at Harka began at 5 a.m. We got thin, lukewarm gruel and then were marched out to our work site. The winter of 1944-45 was extremely severe. The ground was frozen solid. It was almost impossible to sink a shovel into the soil. Yet we did it, otherwise they would have beaten us to death. This went on seven days a week, from five a.m. until six p.m. Afterwards we had to line up for dinner—mostly the same thin gruel with a small piece of rock-hard bread. Since they had no time to build barracks, the Germans requisitioned the unheated barns from the local farmers. We slept on straw, which was also home to fleas, lice, and an assortment of other insects and vermin.

By March of 1945 the eastern sky was routinely lit up by artillery fire and the night air was filled with the droning of Allied bombers passing overhead. One cold March morning at 4:00 a.m. the Vopos (*Volks Polizei*) sounded the alarm and chased us out of the barracks. This time it was not for work. We were ordered to pack in a hurry our meager belongings, line up in formations, and after a breakfast of thin gruel and a slice of bread, start marching.

The Vopos were mostly men over fifty-five, unfit for fighting but good enough to brutally lord it over a bunch of living skeletons. After a couple of hours of forced marching we came to a narrow path. On both sides, men with clubs and rifles were beating us mercilessly. They were members of the Waffen SS. Anyone who fell down and did not get up fast enough was shot on the spot, as were those who tried to escape into the adjacent forest.

Late that afternoon we arrived at our first destination: the little industrial town of Wiener Neustadt, some forty miles south of Vienna and twenty-five miles west of the camp we had left at dawn. The town had been very heavily bombed. At the railway station, which had also been bombed, a long line of cattle cars was waiting for us on a siding. We were hastily and unceremoniously shoved in, eighty to a hundred men to a car. The doors were locked and the train started to move slowly. We had been given no food or water since breakfast.

The train had to go slowly because the tracks were bombed everywhere. It took three days and two long nights for us to travel to Krems, which was only seventy miles west of Vienna. At Krems, our train came to a halt. We were exhausted from lack of sleep and food, having received nothing but a few cups of lukewarm water during the gruelling journey. Krems, an important railway junction, also had been heavily bombed. The damage to the tracks prevented our train from bringing us any closer to our own destination. This, I discovered later, was a great stroke of luck, for our destination was death: we were bound for the infamous Mauthausen concentration camp.

By this time the Vopos, who must have sensed that the Third Reich was unraveling, were beginning to think more about their own problems than about their duties. This too would work to our benefit. We were allowed out of the cattle cars and ordered to sit near the tracks. We were given water, which was drawn from a large tank near the tracks. It was meant for railway engines, but tasted good to us. We still had no food, so we ate the grass and weeds.

The main east-west Highway to Vienna ran parallel with the railroad tracks. On the highway there was a steady stream of people, some going east, others heading west. All of them were carrying suitcases or backpacks, all of them civilians, mostly women, children and old people. We did not know what they were fleeing from, but we could guess: the Allied armies, namely, the Russians from the east and the Americans from the west. These were evacuees returning to their homes, like so many homing pigeons. Walking was the only way to get through those regions where the railroad tracks had been bombed out.

Sitting near the tracks gazing at the mass of human traffic on the road, I suddenly found myself craving after food. I thought: I must try to escape and fill my stomach just one more time with whatever food I can steal or beg. If they catch me and shoot me on the spot, so be it! Just one more meal, food of any kind, and hang the consequences.

I looked down at my clothing. Here was yet more luck. By the time the work camp in Harka was established, the Nazis must have run short of the striped concentration camp uniforms, for they had let us wear our civilian clothes. Mine were by now mostly tattered rags, but they would not give me away. I was, of course, wearing a yellow armband with the Star of David and the word JUDE printed in simulated Hebrew script. To be caught without the armband was punishable by a bullet through the back of the head. But the armband, I knew, would have to go.

My brain started to work. Whatever spare clothing I had in my backpack I traded for an Austrian hat. Then I slipped off the yellow armband. After that, as soon as our guards were not watching my section, I slowly ambled over to the highway and joined the stream of people wandering to and fro. I never turned back. For a long time—an eternity—I feared that a shot would ring out and I would fall by the wayside to die. Miraculously, it never happened. I escaped.

The first group I joined on the highway was an elderly couple. I offered to carry their suitcases from the bombed-out tracks to the makeshift station that had been set up to the east of the damaged area, and from which rail shuttles were carrying passengers east to Vienna. My pay was a big slice of bread and a small slice of home-smoked bacon. I must have made half-a-dozen such trips between the two rail ends, each time offering my services as a porter in exchange for a little food. On one of these trips, I saw a man in striped uniform hauling a handcart loaded with five or six bodies, which were also wearing the same striped clothing. Behind the man pushing the cart was a Vopo carrying a rifle. All the dead had dried blood on their temples. As the food I earned from these trips entered my starved body and my brain started to work better, I became more conscious of my surroundings and the danger that one of the guards might recognize me as I walked by, or that one of my old comrades would call over to me. I had to get out of there, but how? On the trains they had frequent identity checks. Young men without papers, especially those carrying on their bodies the sure-fire identification mark of circumcision, would not survive a trip.

At dusk I was lugging an extremely heavy suitcase for two young women in their late teens or early twenties. They were very pretty and my head told me that at an earlier time, under more favourable conditions, I would have looked longingly at their full bodies, their slim legs and lovely faces. But at that moment my gaze was fixed upon a loaf of bread sticking out from one of their backpacks.

Suddenly a military truck came to a squealing halt behind us. Two men in Waffen SS uniforms yelled out of the cab at the girls, "Where are you going?" The girls answered in unison, "Stockerau!" (a small town north of Vienna). "Hop in," said one SS man, "I can take you as far as Vienna. From there you have to find your own way. By the way," he continued, "the Russians are in the suburbs already, so you better be careful!" I did not wait for a personal invitation. I jumped into the back of the truck and was accepted as an extra piece of luggage travelling with two pretty young women. I knew that the two SS men were not the slightest bit interested in me, which put my heart at ease.

Three hours later we reached Vienna. It was dark, but the eastern sky was glowing with a strange orange light. The steady boom of artillery fire told me that the Red Army's siege of Vienna was in progress. Heavy smoke filled the air. Our driver yelled back from the cab, "Get out now! This is our last stop before we join our unit!"

All three of us jumped out and found ourselves standing in a dimly lit intersection. The girls quickly disappeared into the darkness. Before I could make up my mind which way to go, an exploding artillery shell knocked me down, leaving me unconscious on the pavement. When I came to my senses, a middle-aged woman was bending over me and asking in Hungarian whether I was hurt. I was dazed and very confused. All I could think was, what is this woman doing, speaking Hungarian to me here in Vienna? Finally I mustered the sense to ask whether there was a hospital nearby. She pointed toward a bluish light approximately a hundred yards away. I thanked her and got up. Except for a few bruises, I was not seriously hurt, so I was able to walk slowly towards the light.

I soon found myself in the Alser-Strasse Hospital. Located in the city's 9th District, it was very busy. A steady stream of patients flowed in, some with bloody home-made bandages, some limping on their own, some carried in by others. The Roman Catholic nuns who ran the hospital did not have the time or the resources to perform administrative duties. They asked no questions; they simply put me down on a cot in one of the corridors, then gave me some thin soup and a loaf of bread. For the next forty-eight hours they did not even look at me. This was exactly what I was hoping for. As a matter of fact, I tried to make myself totally invisible, desperate as I was to avoid the attention of the German soldiers who came through the corridors periodically.

Three days after I was admitted, the nuns finally discovered me, which was a mixed blessing. The first thing they wanted to do was give me a bath. I welcomed the bath, but politely declined the help they so willingly offered. I did not want, at that late stage of the game, to let anyone spot the mark of Abraham! I had barely finished the bath and crawled back on to my cot when a troop of Waffen SS entered the hospital. I could hear their boots clang as they passed by my cot. I covered myself from head to toe with my bedding. From my makeshift hiding place I could hear one of the soldiers talking to the nuns. They told him, "There will be no fighting here," and remained firm, God bless them! After a tense ten to fifteen minutes, the SS left.

One hour later the first Russian soldiers appeared. When I saw them, I thought, "I am a free man again!" Excited by this idea, I hastily got dressed. My nurse tried to persuade me to stay for a few more days in order to fully recuperate, but I would not listen. Worried that the SS might counterattack at any moment and recapture the hospital, I assured her that I felt just fine and left in a hurry. The scene outside the hospital was surreal. Russian artillery manned by troops from central Asia rumbled along the spectacular Ring Strasse. Horses pulled wagons carrying field kitchens, ammunition and bales of hay. Pianos hauled out from fashionable apartment buildings sat on the sidewalks with their lids propped open to accommodate the oats that had been dumped in to feed the horses. Tommygun-wielding soldiers were riding on looted bicycles, taking care to avoid the consequences of the fighting: bombcraters, smoking ruins, dead horses, broken glass and, here and there, dead bodies.

It suddenly dawned on me that my newly found freedom carried new dangers and risks. After all, I was a draft age young man in civilian clothes with no identification papers of any kind. I could be mistaken for a Nazi soldier or spy on the lam. I wondered for a moment about what to do. Then a brilliant idea crossed my mind. On my flight from Krems to Vienna I had saved my yellow armband bearing the Star of David. Now, I thought, instead of condemning me to abuse, slavery or death, this armband will be my passport to life and freedom. After all, the Russians must know that we Jews have been victims of the Third Reich and that our sympathies must be with the liberating Red Army.

This crystal clear logic encouraged me to put on the hated yellow armband one more time, this time voluntarily. But shortly a young Ukrainian conscript stepped in front of me, his Kalishnikov rifle dangling from his shoulders and a looted tripod in his right hand. He yelled, "*Davay Tchasi!*" (Give me your watch!) I tried to explain to him in broken Russian that I had no watch, that I was Jewish, had just escaped from a concentration camp and was heading home to Budapest. As I spoke, I pointed to my yellow armband. The reaction I got was not what I was looking for. His face turned crimson red with hate and anger, and he started yelling, "*Yevrey yup tvoi matj*" (Motherfucking Jew), while beating me with the tripod. I was half dead from the beating when a young man wearing a typical Austrian Loden jacket came over to help me up. He had been watching the whole scene from across the street and stated what had become painfully obvious to me: the yellow armband would not endear me to the Red Army.

The young man told me his name was Hubert. He was 16 years old and also Jewish. During the war he had been hidden by his parent's Aryan doctor, with whom he was still staying. He had no idea what had happened to his parents. Without hesitation, he invited me to stay with him and the doctor until I could safely arrange my trip home to Budapest.

Their apartment was located in an upper-middle-class area of the 6th District off the Mariahilfer-Strasse, once one of Vienna's main shopping streets. Over the next while, Hubert and the doctor gave me a place to sleep, shared their food, and let me use their bathroom where I was able to enjoy the unexpected luxury of soaking in a tub of warm water! I was filled with deep gratitude towards both of them and decided that I must repay them for their gracious hospitality.

But how could a penniless escapee from a forced labour camp, reciprocate? The answer was really quite apparent, since it was being played out daily before my eyes in the streets of Vienna. For whatever reason, the Viennese did not seem (in spite of their Nazi past) to be afraid of the Red Army occupying their city. As a matter of fact they found it quite convenient to go "shopping with Ivan." They would go looking for individual soldiers sightseeing in the once elegant downtown 1st District. They would point out to such soldiers warehouses, boarded up stores, cellars brimming with food and liquor. Then they would give the soldier a bottle of booze and ask him to kindly open up the premises with an ax or a rifle butt or a boot through the door. After that task was performed, the looting began. There was no civilian police, so the Soviet Army had a free hand to loot and rape in the first few weeks after the capture of the city. The looters were a mixed bag of people, mostly working-class, some foreign workers and some, like me, escapees from prisons or camps. None of us had a bad conscience. After all, we were the victims of a cruel and unforgiving Nazi dictatorship. The Viennese referred to the booty as belonging to the "Bonzen," the bosses or the elite of the hated Nazi regime, which had deprived us of all our material possessions and, if the war had continued for just a few more weeks, would have deprived us of our lives too.

My hosts, being law-abiding citizens, did not partake in the looting. Their food supply, however, was running low and needed replacement. I also needed food, not to mention clothes and shoes. So I repaid them for their hospitality (and helped to look after my own needs) by going looting with all the rest. My hosts had no qualms about accepting what I managed to bring home, although they knew perfectly well where it came from.

I stayed with Hubert and the doctor for a couple of weeks. I had to build up my strength before undertaking the trip home to Budapest. In order to do that I had to put on some weight. When I arrived in Vienna I weighed only one hundred pounds, eighty pounds below my normal weight. Preoccupied as I was with getting healthy and with my daily "shopping excursions," I failed to notice something important about my gracious hosts, but I became fully aware of it one night when I woke to find their two bodies pressing against me in my bed. As a confirmed heterosexual, I wanted out of there as fast as possible. I jumped out of bed and locked myself in the bathroom. The next morning, as soon as the curfew was lifted, I thanked them for their hospitality, said goodbye, and left.

I travelled light, taking with me only the new clothes I wore, a pair of workman's overalls, whatever food I could carry in my backpack, plus two bottles of schnapps and several packages of cigarettes for bribing my way safely to Budapest. Having been unable to obtain papers during my stay in Vienna, I travelled without identification.

The distance between Vienna and Budapest is approximately 220 kilometres. The journey in peace-time, including the obligatory stop for border controls, takes four hours by train or three hours by car. My journey, undertaken during the final days of the war, would take a full six days. There was no scheduled transportation between Austria and Hungary; rail lines were bombed out everywhere, as were the highways. The Russian military had total control over all modes of transportation.

The first leg of my trip, to the Hungarian border town of Sopron, was relatively easy. On the eastern out-skirts of Vienna a Russian truck driver gave me a lift in exchange for one bottle of schnapps. He dropped me off in front of the Kommandatura a couple hours later. My enquiry there for another transport to Budapest was met with stony silence. I was made to wait for a German- or

Hungarian-speaking Russian officer. He finally arrived in the late afternoon and told me that I would have to go to a distribution camp for documentation before I could receive my travel papers. Having learned from my Vienna experience with the tripod-wielding soldier, I did not want to dwell on my Jewish origin in order to elicit more sympathy.

I was soon escorted to an international camp on the outskirts of Sopron. The inmates there were mainly British and US ex-prisoners of war waiting for repatriation and workers from all German Occupied Lands: Greeks, Italians, Dutch, Belgians, Frenchmen, Croats, Norwegians, Danes, etc. There was also a small contingent of ex-concentration camp inmates of both sexes, as well as some soldiers from the retreating Hungarian Army. We were guarded by Tito partisans. I learned pretty fast that they ranked the Hungarians lowest on the totem pole of nations, whether they were Jewish or not. Within hours I found out from the ever-humming rumour mills that we would be the very last to be repatriated—if repatriation ever would take place. There was a good possibility of being transported to a Siberian work camp. The Russians had suffered very heavy casualties during the war, and since most of their able-bodied men were still on the eastern front, they were in dire need of labourers. Needless to say, after escaping the Nazis I certainly did not want to be recruited into a Russian Gulag.

Soon after my arrival, I noticed that there were railway tracks leading into the camp. Before nightfall a huge engine steamed in pulling a few third class railcars. The crew of the train was Hungarian. I put on my workman's overalls and befriended the engineer. My second bottle of schnapps and the looted cigarettes assured me the position of a coal-stoker.

The train pulled out of the camp at midnight. The Yugoslav partisan guards, seeing me in overalls, took me to be a member of the crew. I do not remember much of this journey other than it took six days and that I shovelled coal all the way from Sopron to Budapest. There were frequent stops. We took on passengers here and there, mostly peasants bringing food to the cities, some black marketeers, some returnees. Russian soldiers boarded the train at every major junction. At some stations all civilian male passengers were herded off the train—who knows where they wound up.

I was very thankful that I was able to pretend to be one of the crew, since it not only allowed me to get to Budapest but allowed me to enjoy the odd perk. At one stop a Russian officer came over to the locomotive with a big bottle of vodka and thanked us for our efforts to keep the train moving. We drank several toasts with him, to Stalin, to the comrade Major, the glorious Red Army, and to all the Hungarian rail crews who were now part of the great Soviet Empire and therefore *Tovarish-chi!* (comrades).

It was 6:00 a.m. when our train finally came to a halt on the Kelenfoeld Marshalling Yards, some eight kilometres outside of Budapest. This was as close as the train could get, since all major railway stations were bombed out. I would have to walk from Kelenfoeld to our apartment downtown in the 5th District. Three hours later I arrived at my destination. To this day I consider that walk the longest and most agonizing one I have ever undertaken.

The time was mid-April, two months after the fall of Budapest. It was a year-and-a-half earlier, at Christmas time in 1943, that I had last seen my parents and said goodbye to my sweetheart during the two-day furlough I had received unexpectedly. It was the last time I had seen Budapest untouched by the war. The last mail I had received from home was in June of 1944. It was a heavily censored letter that told me my father had passed away due to a bleeding ulcer. Who and what will wait for me now, I wondered as I walked. And who is still alive?

The road leading into the city, which followed the shores of the Danube, certainly did not build up my hopes. Destruction was everywhere, the result of six weeks of street fighting and aerial bombardment. All five major bridges across the Danube had been destroyed by the retreating Nazi troops, who gave no warning to the civilian traffic crossing the bridges in streetcars, on bicycles, or on foot. The landmark Royal Palace, located on a commanding hill on the Buda side, was in ruins. So was the elegant Korzo, a favourite and fashionable waterfront promenade that had been the Champs Elysée and Via Veneto of Budapest.

The elegant hotels, coffeehouses, espresso bars and restaurants were in ruins, some of them boarded up, the gilded signs hanging forlornly from their masts, banging in the cold April wind. Here and there some of the buildings that had escaped the destruction sported the Soviet flag with its hammer and sickle. The gothic Parliament Building, which had also suffered heavy damage, was now crowned with a giant red star. Ruins and bomb craters were everywhere, but civilians were nowhere to be found. Occasionally a troop of Red Army soldiers marched past on a deserted street, singing in unison, "*Hey Katyusha....*" Unlike Vienna, I could see no crowds "shopping with Ivan," only an oppressive black cloud of doom hanging over a once-vibrant city.

As I crossed the main circular boulevard called Lipot Korut, which was not far from our apartment, my spirits recovered somewhat: the destruction was not quite as bad as elsewhere. Five minutes later, having passed through the familiar streets of my youth, I was delighted to see our building standing all in one piece except for a few chunks of plaster knocked out by some errant bullets.

I rang the bell. Soon I heard my mother's voice call, "Who is it?" Filled with emotion, I was speechless. She looked through the peephole and cried out my nickname, "Pista, Pista!" I was home at last!!!

After all the hugs and tearful kisses, I asked her, "Mother, what do you know about Eva?" Her face dropped and I feared the worst. Then, trying hard to maintain a tone of voice that would not betray her disapproval of my one and only love, she said: "She is okay, living close by. I hope I can find her address. I must have written it down somewhere."

At that moment I sensed that although all three of us had come out of the Holocaust alive, my mother was still unable to forgive her son for sharing his love with another woman. And she would remain that way to the end of her life.

# 4

## ESCAPE FROM THE SOVIETS

S everal weeks later, on August 15th, 1945, Eva and I were married before a magistrate at the 5th District Office. It was a simple ceremony, held in a small room that reeked of pipe tobacco. Four people were present: the two of us; Gyuri, our friend and witness; and the magistrate, who had a hare lip. Eva, Gyuri and I had to make great efforts to keep a straight face while the magistrate solemnly recited the marriage vows. There was no reception, no music, no in-laws, parents or family of any kind. Six years of war and misery had not taught our parents that when a man and a woman love each other deeply and make a commitment to each other, no one has the right to interfere. To the day of their death neither my mother nor my father-in-law could forgive us for loving each other.

Right after the ceremony we had a modest lunch at a nearby restaurant. While we were eating, a group of drunken Soviet officers began to make passes at my new bride. I paid the bill and we left in a hurry. Though it was six months after the war had ended in Hungary, it was not wise to get into a fight with members of the Red Army. After our hasty departure from the restaurant, Eva and I went home to our respective parents without saying a word about being married. In light of the oppressive presence of the Soviets and the opposition of our parents, ours was an impossible and painful situation. We had to leave Hungary, and leave soon. Our plan was simple: get out of Hungary, cross southern Austria into Italy, head for a port city, and get on a ship that would take us overseas. Overseas was a very rosy but vague destination that included North and South America, Australia, and some British and French colonies in Africa. We were so cocksure of ourselves that the idea of failing never occurred to us. After all, we had survived the war, Nazi Germany and the Holocaust. And, so far at least, we had managed to weather the Soviet occupation and the hostility of our parents. Furthermore, we spoke several languages and I had a trade and a high school diploma. More importantly still, neither of us would shy away from any honest job offered to us.

On the morning of September 7th, a brilliant late-summer day, we went to the waiting room of the Southern Railway Station and met a group of people who, like ourselves, were determined to leave Hungary. Our leader, a young man in his late twenties, gave us a briefing. Our cover story was that we were a group of Polish Jews in transit through Hungary, destined for Palestine. No Hungarian was to be spoken. This was tough for a great number in our party since Hungarian was the only language they knew. Anyone who could not speak Polish was ordered to play deaf and dumb. All of us, Polish-speaking or not, had to destroy any papers we had in our possession, since these would have identified us as Hungarians.

By this time a semblance of order had returned to the country. The trains, for example, were running on time. Thus our journey to Szentgothard, a dull little town on the Austrian border, took only eight hours. We shared a third-class compartment with a newly married middle-aged couple named John and Mary. It was a second marriage for both of them, having lost their previous spouses in the Holocaust. They were very much in love and bubbled with enthusiasm and hope for a new beginning in some distant land, any land, but preferably overseas, far away from the destruction and despair that characterized post-war Europe. They were excellent company for Eva and me.

After our uneventful train trip had brought us to Szentgothard, our leader and guide assembled his ragtag band of bogus Polish refugees, some with babes in arms, all lugging belongings of one kind or another. Together we started walking toward the Austrian frontier.

Our first border crossing was the easiest, since it was from Soviet-occupied Hungary to Soviet-occupied Austria. When we arrived at the border, there were four newly recruited Hungarian guards sitting outside their post playing a card game. They did not even look up as our group of approximately sixty persons marched into Austria. There was no corresponding Austrian customs hut on the other side of the border because of the Allies' plan to divide Austria, like Germany, into four zones of occupation. The Soviets received Lower Austria, parts of Upper Austria and, most importantly, the province of Burgenland, a narrow strip of land, some thirty to fifty kilometres wide, running along the eastern border of Austria. Having control of Burgenland, the Soviets effectively cut off Hungary and the other newly occupied satellites from any contact with the West.

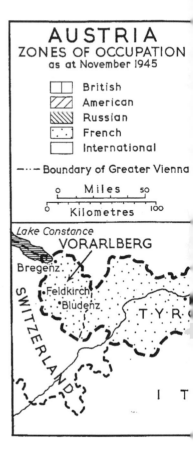

**AUSTRIA**
ZONES OF OCCUPATION
as at November 1945

British
American
Russian
French
International

—·· — Boundary of Greater Vienna

o Miles 50
o Kilometres 100

*Lake Constance*
VORARLBERG
Bregenz
Feldkirch
Bludenz
SWITZERLAND
T·Y·R·
I·T

Map of occupied **Austria**

Our second and more important border-crossing lay ahead: the demarcation line separating the Soviet Zone of Austria from the British Zone. This border, which was thirty kilometres from the point at which we had entered Burgenland, was heavily guarded on both sides. Our guide kept us in the dark about this fact, probably thinking the less we knew the better. Soon after

entering Burgenland late in the afternoon, we left the main road. Under the cover of growing darkness, we crossed over farms and open fields, passing barns and grazing animals.

After some hours walking across the Austrian countryside, our guide led us along forest trails into the foothills of the Alps. Sometimes we paused for thirty to forty minutes in hushed silence, waiting for a Russian patrol to pass. Once a baby cried, then stopped, and to this day we do not know whether someone strangled that baby to prevent it from giving us away. All through the night we heard whistles, short guttural Russian commands, dogs barking, and roosters crowing. We marched between periods of rest that got shorter as the pace grew more hectic. Our suitcases felt heavier and heavier.

It must have been about 3:00 or 4:00 a.m. when Eva and I realized that we had somehow lost the group. We were exhausted and thirsty, alone in the middle of a pitch black forest. We could see or hear no sign of any of our fellow escapees. Since there was really nothing else we could do, we thought we might as well sit down and rest for a while. We had to gather up our strength. At daybreak we would find out where the sun rose and head in the opposite direction to reach our destination.

Taking sustenance from that thought, and from the last of our drinking water, we heard voices, *Hungarian* voices! We soon discovered a group of Hungarian soldiers struggling through the bush. After weary greetings, they told us they were heading home from a British POW camp. We showed them the trail leading back to Hungary, and in turn, they pointed towards a narrow road at the bottom of a hill some two miles away. In the growing grey light of dawn, we saw a lone Tommy passing by on a motorcycle: Hallelujah! It was the British Zone! We thanked the soldiers, wished them good luck, then dropped our heavy suitcases right there in the middle of nowhere and started running downhill toward the road. We did not even think of Russian patrols. The sight of the lone Tommy gave us courage and strength. Two hours later we checked in at the British military post in Fuerstenfeld, Styria.

As I said before, we were young, foolish, naive, full of piss and vinegar and self-confidence. We were penniless refugees without passports, joining millions of displaced persons (DPs) like ourselves who were roaming through the ruins of post-war Europe—yet we did not doubt for a moment that we would reach our goal. No one, of course, really wanted us and the other millions of DPs, except Stalin, who was anxious to get his ex-subjects back. For the victorious Allies, we represented a big fat headache. What were they to do with these masses that included ex-POWs, traitors, quislings, and ex-slave laborers of Nazi Germany. It must have been tempting to send us all back where we came from. Alas, some unfortunate ones were indeed sent back. Meanwhile giant DP camps were opened up to house, feed and process all the rest.

The British commander of Fuerstenfeld put us on a truck that brought us to the largest DP camp in Styria: Kapfenberg-St. Marein. Here we met up again with John and Mary, the couple with whom we had shared the train ride from Budapest to the border. The four of us still had similar ideas about getting overseas, so we decided to move on together toward the Italian border. Since Kapfenberg was a newly opened camp where total chaos reigned, our departure was simple. After receiving some food, we just left.

A military truck gave us a lift to nearby Bruck an der Mur where we managed to get a deluxe room at a local hotel. How and why we managed that is still a total mystery to me, as the town was full of people, both military and civilian. Our train to Klagenfurt departed the next morning at 5:30 a.m. My wife was most reluctant to leave that wonderful, princely accommodation—the wall-to-wall carpet, the fresh linen on the bed, the heavy terrycloth towels and the huge bathtub that could accommodate two people. I sympathized, but we had to push on. After a wonderful hot bath, the four of us boarded the train for Klagenfurt. Italy, here we come!!!

Klagenfurt, the capital of the southernmost Austrian province of Carinthia (Kaernten), was in those times the Casablanca of Central Europe. I mean the Casablanca of the classic movie with Ingrid Bergman and Bogie and Sidney Greenstreet. Shady characters, black marketeers, spies, refugees, ex-Nazis, political outcasts from Tito's Yugoslavia were all over the place. We headed to one of the big coffeehouses downtown. Our goal was to find out how to get across to Italy. Upon arrival, John and Mary met a hometown friend who told us that we were in luck: the British military was assembling a transport of Turkish and Albanian refugees to repatriate via Italy. All we had to do was report to British Headquarters and register as Turks. If we succeeded in doing that, the British would put us on a train to Italy within a few days. Then, after arriving in any of the country's major cities, we would step off the train, get to a port, find a ship going overseas, and *pronto....* It all sounded so simple, but the execution of it proved rather complicated.

The very first part was simple enough. The British military section in charge of refugees was located in a former Klagenfurt orphanage. We entered the forbiddingly grubby old brick building and were ushered into a barren room where the only adornment was a picture of King George VI, the reigning British monarch. The master sergeant in charge pulled out a registration form and wrote down all the bullshit I fed to him. I borrowed the story of a schoolmate of mine whom we all had envied. Why? Because when roll-call was made and we had to recite the place of our birth, he was the only one who came from a romantic and exotic city: Istanbul! The rest of us were all from Budapest, which seemed mundane.

The schoolmate in question, Steven G., had a Turkish father and a Hungarian mother. His parents divorced while he was an infant, and his mother took him back to Hungary. He did not speak or understand Turkish. Neither did I. That was why his story was so useful to me. As far as my wife Eva was concerned, we did not have to fib at all. She was registered under her own maiden name as being married to a Turkish national, that is, me. Officially speaking my name was now Ertoglu, the Turkish equivalent of my schoolmate's name. At least I thought it was the Turkish equivalent. To this day I'm not entirely sure. In any case, the name stuck to me like molasses for nearly three years.

As soon as we had our new identity secured, we began to look forward to meeting the other members of the Turkish transport. We expected them to be young refugees from Hungary or Czechoslovakia and like ourselves, intending to emigrate overseas. When a young corporal escorted us to a classroom that had been converted into a dormitory and we met the other "Turks," we were surprised to discover that they really were ethnic Turks, not from Turkey, mind you, but from the southern regions of the Soviet Union. They included Chechens, Tadjiks, Khazaks, Tartars, Uzbekhs, and Azeris captured during the German blitzkrieg and brought to Germany. Some of them were recruited into the Mohammedan SS set up by the Germans, others were "guest workers." None of them wanted to return to the Soviet Union, where they would face either a bullet in the head or the Gulag. They were therefore pleased that Turkey, which had remained neutral during the War, was willing to give asylum to all ethnic Turks who wished to go there. Turkey, however, was in no hurry to admit any and every ethnic Turk. It was happy to let the British sort out the criminals, especially the war criminals.

Eva and I got a double bed in the middle of that huge dormitory, as did John and Mary who did not give a hoot about their surroundings. Ignoring the piercing black eyes of our "fellow Turks," they got down to some very serious lovemaking. Though a grey blanket covered them, there was no mistaking the sounds—the groans, the little shrieks of joy—not to mention the rhythm of the blanket. We felt very embarrassed, I don't know why. Yet amazingly, none of our mostly young male room-mates seemed to mind or even notice.

Next morning we received some sad news: there would be no transport to Italy! As it turned out, the previous transport, comprised mostly of young Central European refugees, had vanished in Udine. Consequently, the British military decided to place all refugees—Turks, Serbs, Croats, Bosnian Muslims, Czechs, Belgians, Swiss—in a big DP camp some ten kilometres from Klagenfurt.

Camp Waidmansdorf, located on the shores of picturesque Woerther-See and run by the British military, became home to 3,500 DPs of forty-five different nationalities. The commanding officer was Major Oxborrow, a dashing Scot. Hollywood could not have cast a better British officer. The sign on his private quarters proclaimed: "THE MOST DISPLACED." This suggested that he did not particularly enjoy the posting given to him after his service on various fronts with the British 8th Army, but as a good soldier he shouldered his new duties well. His biggest problem was the language barrier. Except for the administrator, Mrs. Carstairs, who spoke a little German, there was nobody on the British staff who spoke any of the inmates' mother tongues.

I had only a superficial knowledge of English, but enough to be picked for important camp jobs. Eva, whose English was much better than mine, was selected to work under Mrs. Carstairs in camp administration. The two women did not like each other very much, which was no great wonder as Mrs. Carstairs was a typical British upper-class snob who very early on suspected that our Turkish refugee story was bogus.

When the British began to recruit truck drivers to service the camp, I volunteered and was quickly accepted. My previous experience consisted of driving my uncle's delivery van to the Great Market of Budapest in the morning and picking up the various fruits needed for the day's baking. On the morning of my second day at work, when it was raining miserably, I had to hit my brakes hard in order to avoid colliding with a cyclist. The van slid across the wet cobblestones into the oncoming traffic, which included a horse-drawn wagon. Luckily the two huge Clydesdale horses parted and the wagon mast missed me by half an inch when it broke through the windshield. I was also lucky that my truck's mudguard neatly shaved the horses' legs without drawing a drop of blood. That near miss, which occurred in 1941, was the last time I had driven any vehicle.

My first assignment at Waidmansdorf was to pick up a load of straw from some farmers in the foothills of the southern Alps. Actually the farms were located at a summit serviced only by a very poor, narrow logging road. My three-ton truck had bravely made it to the top when the engine suddenly died without provocation. There were no phones anywhere. What could I do? It was too far to walk back to the camp. So I spent the night in a farmer's barn. The next morning two jeeps came to my rescue. Later I learned that my wife Eva had made such a scene when I failed to return on time that they came after me at the first light of dawn.

That first fiasco, strangely enough, earned me a promotion. Thanks to my lousy driving and my scant knowledge of English, I became the transport chief and dispatcher for the camp. Sixteen Yugoslav truck drivers were assigned to my care. The drivers were mostly Croats and Bosnian Muslims, the mechanics were Slovens. One thing they had in common was a tremendous capacity for guzzling down any liquor they came across. Another was swearing. The Serbo-Croat language has evolved a rich and varied vocabulary of profanities and obscenities. I have not to this day come across any other language in which you could swear for a half an hour without ever repeating yourself. As I did not really speak Serb-Croatian, my drivers and mechanics and I conversed in German, the *lingua franca* of Central Europe, a language we all hated yet all understood and spoke to various degrees. But I quickly picked up the most common swear words in Serbo-Croatian, which immediately established a warm bond and trust between my drivers and me. Whenever something went wrong and I let loose with a string of profanities, they would respectfully stand at attention, listening cheerfully and occasionally correcting me. They were totally devoted to me, and they followed my commands faithfully. They were also excellent drivers and great mechanics.

At one time the Austrian police reported to the British camp authorities that farmers in the neighbouring villages were being robbed and assaulted by roving bands of Yugoslav men driving British military trucks. We conducted a serious investigation to find the culprits, which did not lead anywhere. No one would snitch on a comrade. But from that day on, every evening the drivers had to surrender not only their ignition keys but also their distributor heads, and all had to carry a log book recording their daily runs and mileages so that their fuel consumption could be monitored. These measures slowed down their activities somewhat, but did not totally stop the night raids.

My wife and I enjoyed a privileged position in the camp. We were given a separate barrack for our living quarters, which I also used for my dispatch office. We had a private bedroom and bathroom, which was an unheard of luxury. Eva was in charge of a camp store, the profits from which were plowed back into sporting and cultural activities: soccer games, musical evenings, theatrical plays, etc.

Both of us were deeply involved in our work, but we had free time for excursions in my jeep into the beautiful alpine countryside. We visited the nearby Schloss Hochosterwitz, which is the castle Walt Disney used as a his model for the castle in *Sleeping Beauty*. We also went into Klagenfurt occasionally to see a movie. The first time we went, we had an emotional experience that I have not been able to forget to this day. After the film, "God Save the King" was played on the speakers. To the great dismay of some members of the audience, who tried to sneak out when the last film credits were rolled, everyone—military and civilians alike—would stand at attention. We were probably the only ones in the audience who felt a great surge of emotion at this moment. For those of us who had been cut off from all Western music, hymns, films, theatre, books, magazines, newspapers for the past decade, the song was the sound of freedom. We clutched each other's hands and stood at attention until the last strands of music faded away. I glanced at Eva through my own tear-filled eyes. She was crying too. Two months after leaving Hungary, it finally sunk in: We were free at last!

This was by no means the only time that we encountered politically charged material at the cinema. The Allies were trying to re-educate the Austrians, or maybe just remind them of their collective guilt because of their

Camp **Commandant van de Cooke** (driving)
and assistants, Camp Waidmansdorf, Austria (British Zone),
1946

participation in the atrocities committed by the Third
Reich. Thus, before each feature film we saw in
Klagenfurt, we were shown documentaries of Auschwitz,
Buchenwald and Mauthausen. No details were spared.
We saw it all: the barely living skeletons, the thousands
of corpses, the gas chambers and the crematoria. I, who
had been an inmate not too long before, fainted dead
away in the middle of one documentary. I had to get out
into the fresh air to assure myself that the nightmare was
over. Such documentaries gave me nightmares; the smell
of death surrounded me everywhere.

In early fall of 1946, the British Military handed over
the camp to the UNRRA (United Nations Relief &
Rehabilitation Agency). Major Oxborrow, who I think
had a crush on my wife, gave a tearful farewell party.

As he danced with Eva, who perhaps had a mild crush on the major, I had pangs of jealousy and felt relieved that there was a change in command.

The new UNRRA camp director was a pipe-smoking Dutchman by the name of Captain Van de Cooke. As a civilian he had been captain of a canal barge in Holland. Like him, the whole UNRRA team was quite inexperienced, but full of goodwill. They were a mixed bag: De Cooke's deputy was an American, the camp doctor was a Swiss-German woman, the supply officers were Canadian, and the secretary was a Jewish woman from Scotland. Mrs. Carstairs stayed on and received an UNRRA badge as an intelligence officer. Except for Mrs. Carstairs, the UNRRA staff relied heavily on the inmate leaders, which included Eva and I, a nervous little Greek administrator by the name of Costas, and an Estonian camp police chief by the name of Heino, who had a special talent as a woodcarver. We four more or less were running the show.

In fact, we were so involved in our duties in the camp that we temporarily lost sight of our goal of getting overseas. Although we knew that there was no future for us in Austria, we were making only the feeblest efforts to emigrate. Just as we realized that we needed to make a change, two events occurred that shook us out of our comfortable existence.

The first arrived one morning when Mrs. Carstairs approached me and asked that I become the leader of the Turks in the camp. I suspected a clever ploy on her part to unmask our phony claim to Turkish status, one I would have gladly abandoned if I only could. But reverting to being Hungarian would have gotten us two very unpalatable choices: (1) a fast repatriation or (2) transfer to a special camp for ex-enemies of the Allies, something very much like a POW camp, which would have been full of ex-nazis. I stalled by making noises that such an honour should be bestowed to one of the elders "according to our ethnic tradition." She did not buy this, but told me confidentially that within the next few days the long-awaited Turkish liaison officer would be arriving and setting up a repatriation scheme. She was hoping that I would help both her and the emissary from Ankara.

The second event that helped bring our stay in the camp to an end occurred that same day. Captain van De Cooke approached Eva and informed her that he wanted the two of us to help him to organize a new camp in Kapfenberg-St. Marein, where he has been appointed camp director. We jumped at this opportunity, not only because it allowed us to avoid a final confrontation with Mrs. Carstairs, but also because we were told that a great influx of mostly Jewish Central European refugees were expected at the new camp. What a relief it would be to say goodbye to the Turks, the Yugoslavs and the Estonians, who were mostly Nazi collaborators, wild characters who carried long daggers in their boots. And what a pleasure, to be with like-minded people from a civilized society. The fact that Mrs. Carstairs would stay behind in Camp Waidmansdorf was an extra bonus. On the other hand, the loyalty of my crew was touching to say the least: the drivers and mechanics all wanted to come with me to St. Marein. However, the new UNRRA policy was to segregate the refugees according to nationalities, so they had to stay behind.

The inmates at Camp Kapfenberg-St. Marein, located near Bruck an der Mur, were mostly Polish Jews who had spent the war years in Siberia after the eastern part of Poland was occupied by the Red Army, following the infamous 1939 Pact between Hitler and Stalin. They had had a hard life in Siberia. Their only blessing was that they had managed to escape the extermination camps of the Nazis. The Soviet system, however, had turned them into battle-hardened practitioners of the survival of the fittest.

I discovered this one day when I sent a couple of trucks into the camp to pick up the pregnant women and the sick children for a medical checkup in the camp hospital. To my dismay, young toughs kicked the women and children off the trucks and went for a joyride. In order to prevent this from happening again, our Swiss doctor had to come in her Jeep with a gun pointed at the young toughs as she visited the sick. These same young Mafioso routinely stole the extra rations meant for the sick and the infirm. Their brutality made me want to leave St. Marein for Vienna.

Another incident gave me a push in the same direction. In early October of 1946, when the first frost descended, the camp allocated part of an adjacent alder forest for woodcutting to supply fuel for the barracks. The young and able males picked for the job, who were rewarded with extra rations and pay, went on strike the very first day. The remaining crowd blamed the unheated barracks on the camp administration. Frustrated by their lot, they began to riot. To our shame we had to call in military police to restore order, while the crowd inside the barracks chopped up the furniture

**Eva and Steve,**
Vienna, 1947

for firewood and another part of the crowd surrounded the UNRRA officer's quarters, threw rocks, called us Nazis, and asked for our blood. I was on my way to a work site when my jeep was surrounded by an angry mob. They were banging on the hood, rocking the jeep, and had almost succeeded in turning it over when the camp police rescued me. Both Eva and I felt that our very lives were threatened by the people we were longing to be with. And we felt pangs of nostalgia remembering our ex-fellow inmates from camp Waidmansdorf, where we were respected and appreciated. We wanted out.

Fortunately we had a good friend in Miss R., the Jewish woman from Scotland who also worked for the AJDC (American Joint Distribution Committee), a US-based Jewish aid organization. She sensed our disappointment in St. Marein, recommended both of us glowingly to the Vienna headquarters of AJDC, and arranged for our transfer to Vienna. According to her, people like us were badly needed there.

There was only one setback: Vienna, although occupied by all four Allied powers, was deep in the Russian-occupied zone of Austria, in the province of Lower Austria (Nieder-Oesterreich). In order to get there, we would have to risk once again being apprehended by the Soviets we thought and hoped we had left behind for good.

The demarcation line separating British-occupied Styria and Soviet-occupied Nieder-Oesterreich ran through the famous Austrian spa and ski resort of Semmering. When our Jeep pulled up to the Red Army guard post and barrier there, both Eva and I had a queasy feeling in our stomachs. Miss R., who had agreed to

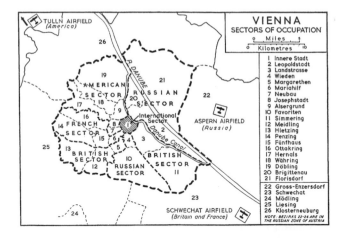

Map of occupied **Vienna**

accompany us, encouraged us to remain calm. The young sentry, with his Kalishnikov slung across his shoulder, took an interminably long time studying our papers and all the required thirteen stamps in our alien passports. We were dressed in British military uniforms with UNRRA badges stitched to our shoulders. He looked us up and down, unsmiling, and with deep suspicion. Finally, at the urging of our Miss R., he waved us through.

As we drove through the beautiful Austrian countryside, we were looking forward with great anticipation to our new life in Vienna. Both Eva and I were city-bred urbanites. Our year in the country had filled us with longing for life in a big city with its theatres, movies, shops, and cafés. Vienna would not disappoint us, though it would postpone considerably our emigration overseas.

The city we encountered when we arrived in Vienna was similar to that portrayed in the movie, *The Third Man.* Though not as heavily damaged as Budapest, the city was scarred by bombed-out buildings (including six-storey concrete bunkers built by the Nazis), mountains of rubble, and torn-up streets. The inhabitants met their material needs by dealing with ration cards, fleamarkets, and blackmarketeers. The streets were crawling with soldiers, ex-Nazis, and spies. Yet the city was exciting and in a strange way, quite enjoyable.

Vienna provided its inhabitants with a great variety of entertainment. There was folk music in the wine gardens of the suburbs, especially in Grinzing and Gumpoldskirchen. There were delightful plays. The great actors of the German theatre, who had returned from exile, prison, or the concentration camps, provided Eva and me with some unforgettable evenings. I will always remember, for example, seeing Thornton Wilder's *Our Town* played by Albert Basserman, Ernst Deutsch, and a teenager by the name of Oskar Werner. And there were also the controversial literary cabarets, a unique Central European art form specializing in political satire and therefore detested by the Nazis and the Soviets alike. Eva and I, however, enjoyed the cabarets a great deal, along with all the other sights and sounds of Vienna.

Vienna, like Berlin, was occupied and administered by the four victorious Allies. The city was divided into four Zones, while the hub, the downtown core surrounded by the Ring-Strasse and the Danube Canal, had a monthly alternating change of guards. Not surprising, this made for some strange transformations in the hub. As soon as the Red Army took over the downtown, for example, the literary cabarets shut down, only to open up again when the command was passed on to one of the Western Allies.

The presence of the Soviets created dangers for us. Totally unbeknownst to us when we accepted our new positions, the NKVD (forerunner of the KGB, the Russian Secret Police) was conducting a campaign of forceful repatriation of all East Europeans whose country was in the Soviet sphere: Poles, Hungarians, Bulgarians, Czechs, etc. They picked up anyone from these countries they could catch travelling out of the Western Zones of the city, whether by car, streetcar, train, bicycle, or on foot. A Romanian acquaintance of ours went out one morning to buy buns for breakfast at a bakery downtown, which was then under the control of the Red Army. He was picked up and never seen again. To this day we do not know what happened to him.

In order to ensure that a similar fate would not befall us, we had to carry a pink picture ID printed in four languages (English, French, Russian and German) and stamped by thirteen different authorities. My identification, incidentally, carried my true identity, since I had abandoned my Turkish registration as a meaningless exercise.

So there we were, on the one hand, enjoying Vienna for its fascinating culture and, on the other, hating it because it was also a prison—a gilded cage consisting of the three Western Zones and the hub, when the Western Allies controlled it. None of these areas, unfortunately, had an airport. And since the whole of the city was located in the Soviet zone of Austria, we were truly trapped. Unable to leave, we made the most of our leisure and our work.

The AJDC put us in charge of a hostel, where all those lucky people with proper visas and sponsors were wiling away their time until their final travel papers arrived, enabling them to emigrate. The hostel, located in the 14th District in the French Zone, was a converted school. Though it was quite primitive, it was a welcome haven for transients who would otherwise have been unable to find any accommodation in the city, partly because the Occupying Powers had taken over all the hotels, and partly because forty percent of the housing stock had been destroyed by the war.

It was not until February of 1948, after we had been in Vienna for sixteen months, that we finally managed to buy, at an exorbitant price, some false Austrian ID papers. With these papers, we could travel freely from one zone to another, so we decided to escape to Salzburg in the American zone. To avert suspicion, we sent all of our heavy luggage to Salzburg by rail before we left ourselves. A few days later, we followed in a local bus. We dressed as the locals did and spoke only when absolutely necessary. Our German was pretty good, but we didn't want to take any chances. Both of us carried a backpack only to make it look as if we were locals.

At the river Enns, which formed the border between the American and the Russian Zones, we came face to face with Soviet border guards once again. The scene was familiar: young, unsmiling Red Army soldiers, Kalishnikovs slung across their chests, ordered all passengers to get out of the bus, form a single file, and stop at the checkpoint. Some of the soldiers then examined the undercarriage of the bus with long mirror-equipped poles and flashlights, while others scrutinized each passenger and his or her papers in agonizing detail. They looked at the picture on the ID paper then examined our faces slowly, repeating the process countless times before finally letting us pass over the bridge.

As I walked across that bridge, which was only one-hundred feet long, I felt exactly as I had three years earlier when I escaped from my Nazi guards at Krems. I sensed those Tommy guns pointing at our backs and I expected at any moment that a burst of machine-gun fire would cut us down. I looked at the other end of the bridge, where a group of smiling GIs were waving to us. We wanted to run towards them, but we knew it would be foolish since it might provoke those stony-faced border guards to open fire. That of course never happened. After what was surely the longest hundred feet we ever traversed, we made it to the American zone. Once there, we swore to ourselves that no matter what opportunities might open up across the Iron Curtain, we would never return until the Soviet Union and its satellites had fallen.

Soon after crossing the Enns, we made it to Salzburg and discovered a picture-postcard city that had escaped the war almost intact. In fact, the American Zone made it look as if the war had never taken place. While in all of the other parts of Austria you needed ration cards to buy food or even to order a meal in a restaurant, here all you needed was money! Working as we were for the AJDC, we had some of our own, which allowed us to live quite well. But we were determined by this time to let neither the charms of Salzburg nor the challenges of our new responsibilities with the AJDC distract us from our goal of emigrating overseas.

Salzburg, being at the cross-roads between East and West, and being separated from the East by a border that was relatively easy to breach, was teaming with refugees from all over Eastern Europe and from all shades of the political spectrum. The patrons of the Cafe Bazaar (located on the shores of the fast-flowing Salzach river not far from the Bishop's Castle and the Dom spires) were typical. They included various groups of Hungarian refugees, distinguished only by the dates they fled the country: the Nazis of late 1944 and early 1945, the small Agrarians of 1946, the Socialists of 1947, the Communists of the first purges early in 1948, and so on. Each of these groups would gather at separate tables, observing each other with great suspicion and never mixing, not even to the extent of talking to each other. Eva and I did not fit into any of these groups. When asked about our past, we answered that we were refugees, having been cast out by our own in-laws. No one believed us, although this was the unvarnished truth.

It was at the Cafe Bazaar that I met the first consul of the Hungarian Embassy in Vienna, who a year earlier had denied me a passport, offering instead a one-way visa back to Hungary. By now he too was a refugee. I also met one of my cousins, who claimed that he had just escaped from Budapest, after being sentenced to death by firing squad. He had been an officer of the dreaded Hungarian Secret Police, known by the acronym AVO. We met only once, as he was visibly worried that I, who chanced to recognize him, might also betray him. After our meeting he disappeared, and I have never heard of him since.

In spite of our resolve to leave Salzburg quickly for some overseas destination, we were soon on the verge of getting mired in the same rut we had fallen into before in Vienna. We both held important senior positions with the AJDC. Eva was the regional office manager, and I became chief accountant for the Western Region, a position I did not particularly enjoy because I had a great suspicion that some officers were lining their pockets at the organization's expense. I was never able to prove it—and I should add that most of the staff was honest and hard-working—yet I had a gut feeling that the day of reckoning would come and I would be the scapegoat.

The refugee situation in the American Zone received a lot more attention than in either Vienna or the British Zone. Commissions arrived almost daily looking for particular groups or professions. They came from Argentina looking for farmers, from the U.K. and the U.S.A. in search of domestics, from Brazil and Chile seeking miners, and from Australia wanting to find tailors, and so on. Somehow we never qualified, even when we seemed an obvious fit, as we were for a position requiring a couple to manage a hotel and restaurant in Algeria. When even that job was taken by people far less qualified than ourselves, Eva got suspicious. Upon investigation she found out that our own director, who was in charge of the whole Salzburg region, had been scuttling our efforts because he wanted to keep us working for his administration. A showdown ensued and we made it clear to him that if he interfered again we would resign our positions. Being dead serious about this, we recorded it in a letter and sent it to him as well as AJDC headquarters in Vienna and New York.

A5099

# CERTIFICATE OF IDENTITY

This certificate is issued to refugees not enjoying in law or in fact the protection of any government, with the approval of the American Section of the Allied Comission for Austria, through the International Refugee Organisation. Its purpose is to serve as a temporary certificate pending the adoption of an International travel document. In no way does it affect the nationality of the bearer

Citizenship: Hungary

**Name** FLORIS, Stefan

**Place and date of birth** Budapest, Hungary-September 21st, 1920

**Wife's name, place and date of birth** Eva(nee Schmidt), Budapest, Hungary, - January 27, 1920

**Present residence** Muenchener Hauptstrasse 38, Salzburg-Rott, Austria

**\*Minors accompanying and ages** - - -

**Date of leaving former country** September 1945

**Reason for leaving** persecution

**Places and dates of concentration camps** different slave labor camps in Galicia and Northern-Hungary, April 1944-November 1944

Harka, Hungary, November 1944-March 1945, deported to C.C. Mauthausen March 1945-May 1945
**Places and dates of D. P. camps or D. P. status**

DP Camp St. Marein, Austria, October 1945-October 1946

DP Camp Goldschlagstrasse, Vienna, Austria, October 1946-February 1948

Salzburg town since February 1948
**Occupation** f u r r i e r **Also** - - -

**Country of destination** C A N A D A

**Countries of transit** Germany

**Height** 180cms **Weight** 90kgs **Eyes** brown **Hair** brown

**Signature:**

The above information has been properly inscribed in my presence.

**Signed:** **Date:** July 1st, 1948

**Office:** P.C.I.R.O. RESETTLEMENT
SALZBURG, AUSTRIA

\*May include children, brothers, sisters, grandchildren, nieces, nephews. If minors are between 16 and 21 years their pictures must be affixed.

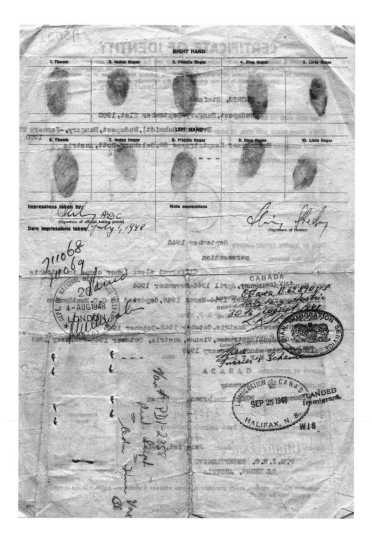

**DP identity papers**
issued by International Refugee Organization,
Salzburg (American Zone), Austria

After we delivered our ultimatum, the next delegation to arrive in Salzburg came from Canada. They were looking for furriers. I felt really dejected, as I did not have the slightest inkling about the fur trade. I told Eva if I was asked a single question on the subject, I would fail the test immediately. She urged me to go anyway, so I went.

When I arrived, I soon discovered that the big gymnasium of the high school was full of instant furriers, hopeful souls who tried to feign superior knowledge of the fur business. Many of them clutched little chunks of fur, held them up and blew into them expertly. Others were trying to sew a couple of fur pieces together. I thought this was really an exercise in futility, since the Canadian furriers would see through this charade instantly. So I sat down with a couple of my friends and started playing Gin Rummy. After a few hands, my name was called. When I reached the interview room, I saw the head of the delegation, a small red-haired man who was obviously quite angry and frustrated. He yelled, "Don't tell me that you are a furrier too!" I was mentally prepared for a question like this, so I said, "No Sir! I haven't got the foggiest idea about the fur business. But I have many other talents, like baking bread and pastry, and making candy. And I never shirk any hard work that is offered to me." He looked at me, stunned. Then he broke into a big grin and said, "This is the first honest man I have seen today!" Turning to the clerks at the desk, he added, "Sign him on!" I could not believe my good luck. I was deliriously happy. When I told Eva about my interview, she hugged me and quietly said, "I told you to go, didn't I?"

**Eva**
entering Halifax Harbour
on board Liberty Ship *General S.D. Sturgis,*
September 25, 1948

Now that we were on the verge of leaving, we realized how much we had both enjoyed Salzburg and its environs: the snowy mountains, the alpine lakes, like the famous Wolfgang See, the charming little alpine villages, the elegant spas like Bad Gastein and Bad Ischl (the retreat of Emperor Franz Joseph), the ski resorts like Zell am See, and the Schafberg where, from the summit, you allegedly could see seventeen lakes. I say "allegedly" because every one of the numerous times we rode the quaint little funicular to the top of the mountain there was either a howling blizzard or pea-soup-like fog.

Salzburg, like Vienna, had provided us with some wonderful theatrical experiences. It was there that we attended a haunting performance of the medieval play *Jederman (Everyman)* in the Dom Square, where we heard the refrain "*Jederman! Jederman!*" echo from the surrounding church spires. And it was there that we attended the *Festspiele* (which had its first season after the war in 1948) and saw *The Magic Flute* played in the Faust Theatre that had been carved out of the rocks. Yes, we had enjoyed Salzburg, that little paradise on earth, a great deal. Yet when the time finally came for us to leave it all behind, we were happy to go. Our new home overseas, which we had been working toward for three years, was calling.

Some four weeks after my interview with the furrier, the final stage of our journey began in a second-class compartment of the Arlberg Express. On the Brenner Pass at the Italian border, we were transferred into cattle cars with *carabinieri* posted in each car. This saddened me, because I had been telling Eva so much about Italy and everything we would see there. I did not anticipate that we would be treated almost like prisoners during our cross-country journey to our embarkation point in Genova. Our best taste of Italian culture along the way was a mortadella sandwich I managed to buy from a vending cart at the great railway station in Milan. We didn't even manage to get a decent view of Genova. I still have the one black and white picture shot there with my box camera showing a small slice of Genova harbour framed by two cattle cars.

The nine day sea voyage on the Liberty Ship: *General S.D. Sturgis* was no luxury cruise, yet I consider it our best cruise as it brought us to our new home. There were 1200 of us DP refugees, each belonging to one of two groups: 800 were single Ukrainian women destined to be domestic servants; 400 were were going to be furriers and tailors. The men were separated from the women. We slept in hammocks, seventy to eighty of us in a series of big rooms. The women had it a little better, being six or eight to a cabin. Meals were served cafeteria style. An American master sergeant was in charge of the galley and kept rushing us through the mealtime with his constant yelling: "Hurry up! Get moving! Go, Go, Go!" My wife got so mad at him on one occasion that she threw down her tray at his feet. Our diet consisted mainly of powdered scrambled eggs, mashed potatoes, and canned meat. Only mothers with young children and pregnant women had the luxury of being served while sitting at a table. I must have been allergic to this food, because during the whole voyage my hands and arms swelled up and were covered with blisters, which eventually turned into an ugly rash.

Other than seeing our first dolphins in the Straits of Gibraltar and weathering the extremely rough waters of the North Atlantic (most passengers were seasick all the time), I don't remember much else about this trip. What I do remember clearly is that, nine days after leaving Italy, Eva and I were standing on the deck when we spotted the land mass of North America. It was a clear day, very windy. Seeing my wife gazing with apprehension towards the distant shore which soon would be our new home, I snapped her photograph. I still cherish that grainy black and white picture, which is worth a thousand words, depicting as it does all the hopes, worries, and expectations of a new arrival in a new country.

Eva
in Winnipeg, November, 1948

# 5

## CANADA

*Ubi bene, ibi patria.* [2]

On September 25, 1948, Halifax Harbour came into view. I spotted a large banner stretched across the dock of Pier 21 saying: WELCOME HOME TO CANADA! I was deeply moved by those four simple words. We had spent three years in various DP camps in Austria and were never welcomed by the locals. Our reduced ration cards were stamped with a capital "A" (meaning *Auslaender* or foreigner), and we were frequently referred to as *verfluchte Auslaender* (Goddam foreigners). But here in Halifax harbour, I could see that beautiful banner: WELCOME HOME TO CANADA. I felt that it contained a personal message welcoming us exclusively! Maybe that banner was not meant for us at all. It was probably for the British war brides or those brave Canadian soldiers returning from the war, the troops whose victory over the forces of Evil had saved our lives. Even so, it made us feel welcome, and so did the Blue Cross ladies who offered us tea and donuts. Oh bless you, Canada, for giving us a home at last!

Our twenty-nine hour ride in the CPR Colonist train to Montreal gave us a perspective of the immense size and diversity of our new country. There on the south shore of the great St. Lawrence river we passed through towns named Rimouski, Rivière du Loup, Mont-Joli, Kamouraska, and many others I can hardly remember anymore. After another two-day train ride, we got to

2. Where life is good for you, there is your homeland.

**Steve**
in Winnipeg, November, 1948

**Eva**
en route to Vancouver, January, 1949

Winnipeg, located roughly midway between the Atlantic and the Pacific. Since this was as far as the Canadian Government of the day paid for our trip, we decided to make our home there.

Thanks to the various aid organizations and unions, we both got jobs within a few days after our arrival. I got work in a candy factory and Eva started out in the garment industry, sewing labels into parkas. We also had no trouble finding accommodation. In spite of this friendly reception, we were not very enthused about life in Winnipeg. The legendary climate, the wind blowing from the North Pole through your bones while you waited for a streetcar on the corner of Portage and Main, made us feel that we were in Siberia rather than Canada. Adding insult to injury was the fact that both my foreman and my wife's boss were Russian. The guttural sound of the language rekindled our memories of the barked commands of the Red Army soldiers in Soviet-occupied Hungary.

One day my wife told me of a conversation she had overheard between a hairdresser and a customer at the beauty parlour. "I listed my house for sale a year ago because we want to move to B.C. and not a bite yet!" said the customer. "What do you think," replied the hairdresser, "if I could sell this crummy business wouldn't I be in Vancouver in an instant!" This conversation convinced us that the right thing to do would be to leave Winnipeg right away, before we acquired any worldly goods, business commitments, or real estate that we probably would not be able to unload in a hurry. From then on we saved all our money for two bus tickets to Vancouver.

With co-workers at the **Bon Ton**
(Steve front row left)

Three months later, on New Year's Eve, 1948, we departed. Four days and three nights later, having crossed over the frozen prairies and the magnificent, snow-covered Rockies, we arrived in Vancouver. Needless to say, it was a miserable rainy day, but it felt like paradise because we were able to stick our noses out without fearing that they would be frozen off.

I settled into my new position at a prestigious pastry shop in downtown Vancouver quite quickly. Eva, however, was not so fortunate. After several failed attempts on the local job market, which included frustrating stints as a bussgirl, a breakfast cook, and a salesgirl, she decided to go into business on her own.

She answered an ad for a partnership in a candy store. The friendly partner, a charming Irishman, turned out to be a drunk. In order to keep her store stocked with homemade candies, I had to work at nights after my nine-hour shift at the pastry shop. Eventually our Irish partner, having a bad conscience, offered to sell us his share in the business at such a good price that we could not refuse. There were definitely advantages to running the store on our own, but working two jobs started to take its toll on me. I begged Eva to sell the business and she reluctantly agreed. Neither of us believed it would be easy.

Eva placed an ad in the paper asking a very high price. A day later a man called Bruce showed up and said he was interested in buying the store—provided I would teach him the art of candymaking. I gladly accepted, not knowing what lay ahead. The following day Bruce arrived with a certified cheque for the full asking price. I immediately took him into the candy kitchen and showed him the intricate procedure for weighing a batch of candies on a commercial scale. Poor Bruce! It took me three hours to get him cleaned up after he got stuck in the glucose barrel. This was the first and last lesson I gave him in candymaking, for it established beyond all doubt the absurdity of trying to teach him the trade. We all agreed that the best thing in the circumstances was for Bruce to hire us to run the business for him. Sometimes, however, even the best thing is not good enough: after four weeks we all gave up. Eva and I began to look for other opportunities.

Like most new arrivals to Vancouver, we had fallen in love with Stanley Park. On one of our Sunday walks there we discovered a little rustic house located near Third Beach, close to the Pauline Johnson Fountain. It was called the Art Gallery Tea Room at Ferguson Point. Sitting at a table, we began dreaming aloud about how much we would love to own such a charming place and what we could do to make it a successful venture, serving hot croissants, European pastries, fancy open-faced sandwiches and, of course, continental lunches and dinners. Overhearing our conversation, the middle-aged lady who seemed to be in charge sat down at our table. "Do you really want to own this place?" she asked. "You can have it, because I certainly do not want it anymore. I have had it up to here! I must have been soft in the head to start this business. This is for young people like yourselves, new immigrants who don't mind working hard seven days a week." That last remark indicated that she had noticed our heavy foreign accents.

We were flabbergasted and could hardly hide our joy at being offered such a great opportunity. With the help of the current owner, Mrs. P.S., we approached the Park Board for a lease. We were enthusiastic enough to offer to sign a percentage lease, one that required us to pay a base of $1200 per year plus 10% of our gross over and above $12,000. Judging from Mrs. P.S.'s business, we thought it would be a very long time before we reached the magic $12,000 mark, at which point the percentage point lease would kick in. (As it happened, we managed to gross over $12,000 during our first year of operation.)

We were in seventh heaven when we got the news that our application for a one-year probationary period was approved. Getting the Tea Room lease turned out to be a double scoop for us, since my mother, who had recently been allowed to leave Hungary, would soon be joining us in Vancouver. And the Tea Room just happened to have two self-contained suites. They were built to accommodate a mess for the officers in charge of the soldiers who manned the shore batteries during the war. We didn't know it at the time, but there was an intricate network of tunnels, concrete bunkers, and barracks at Ferguson Point, not to mention heavy artillery built into the cliffs to guard Vancouver from a Japanese invasion, which of course never materialized. The presence of these defenses explained why the whole western edge of Stanley Park was out of bounds for civilians during the war years.

Our plan was quite simple: Eva, with the help of my mother, would run the restaurant, which we called the Ferguson Point Tea House, while I would keep my job at the pastry shop. We were dreaming of early morning walks in the park, playing tennis, swimming at Third Beach, all the while enjoying the comfort of two spacious, self-contained suites. Eva and my mother, we thought, would make enough money to cover the overhead. Of course things rarely turn out as you dream them. We never walked in the park in the morning, our tennis rackets gathered dust, and we never managed to relax on the beach after an early morning swim. We were far too busy. Eva's wonderful talent for publicity brought us almost instant success. She managed to get interviewed by reporters from all three daily newspapers. They must have seen us as being very exotic and maybe a little nutty for wanting to open a continental sidewalk café in the middle of a rainforest. The public, in any case, ate it up: from then on the only thing we had to worry about was how to cope with the business at hand. My contribution was to quit the pastry shop, which I did right after Easter, and start working full time in the kitchen.

In January of 1951, we started out with our quaint little Tea House, with its magnificent view of English Bay and the mountains of West Vancouver. We soon added four round patio tables and twelve chairs. The wholesaler where we purchased the garden furniture, after learning of our (idiotic) plan, insisted on cash payment upon delivery. But we worked hard and within a few years quadrupled our seating capacity. We succeeded beyond our wildest dreams, in spite of the antiquated liquor laws which made it illegal to serve a drink in Stanley Park. As most restaurateurs know, nobody can turn a profit selling food only! But we managed to prove

**View from Ferguson Point Tea House**,
Stanley Park, Vancouver

"Ferguson Point Tea House" says the split-log sign near Third Beach in Stanley Park. For Vancouver gourmets this means an adventure in dining amid a spectacular scenery setting. It seems incredible that such an exciting retreat is only 15 minutes drive from downtown Vancouver. But scenery isn't enough for Eve and Steve Floris, an adventurous, decorative refugee couple from Budapest. Serving authentic European foods that are reminiscent of the large cafes of European capitals. Hungarian soups that are meaty, spiced and full-bodied; goulashes in rich red gravy; roulades (beef steaks stuffed with onions and rolled with bacon); chicken liver risotto served with rice and Parmesan cheese. Desserts are the pastries the Floris family have been famous for during generations. It's a two-person show. Steve, white chef's hat rakishly a-tilt, cooks. Eve, who hasn't got over a shy dimpling when she smiles is the hostess-waitress. Vancouver diner-outers and tourists who like something different praise the food, scenery and authenticity of Ferguson Point, showplace of Stanley Park.

"Signposts"
by George Vickers

**"Vancouver Guide,"**
Sept. 16 - Sept. 30, 1955

otherwise, although our profits were very small. Even so, we were happy in our work, and happy to be living in Canada.

June 15, 1954 was a proud and joyful day for both Eva and I, a young Hungarian-born couple rejected by their native country, for it was then that we received our Canadian citizenship. Our sponsors were our new friends Bob and Eva Pritchard, whom we had met in the course of our first business venture in Canada (the ill-fated candystore). Although we had been competitors in business, they stood up for us without any hesitation. When the judge asked Bob whether he was acquainted with us, he spoke up and said, "I feel privileged to know them, Sir." This simple statement from a simple working man touched us very deeply. The ceremony took place in the impressive old court house. Judge Sargeant conducted the proceedings and two RCMP officers in traditional red tunics stood by as we took the Oath of Allegiance to her Majesty, Queen Elizabeth the Second.

After that, we worked very hard at the Tea House for another ten years, in spite of the fact that we made very little profit. The story of those years would not be complete without mentioning our three headwaiters, Harry, Bunu, and Ernie; and our souchef, Jimmy. I don't know whether it was because of my wife's charm, the food, the wages, the tips, the unique location in Stanley Park, or the great camaraderie we developed with them, but those four men slogged it through with us over almost all of our fifteen year tenure at the Tea House.

In an industry known for its high staff turnover, their commitment was remarkable, especially since ours was a seasonal business. We had tried initially to keep the Tea House open all year round, but that proved impractical. As soon as the bright days of summer gave wy to rain, drizzle, and fog, visitors simply stopped coming to Stanley Park. So we soon got used to closing the Tea House after the Thanksgiving weekend and opening again in the spring. And year after year our waiters and our souchef returned.

Harry answered our ad when we opened up for our second season in the spring of 1952. The three of us bonded instantly. Having grown up in Vienna, he had great deal of Viennese charm, and a wonderful sense of humour, which made us all laugh on many occasions. One of my favorites occurred on a very hot and sunny afternoon when a half-naked man with a heavy German accent accosted Harry and asked, "Heff you got anythink against sun burn?" "No!" answered Harry, "I am totally in favour of it!" He was also a very hard worker. Our customers, both male and female, ate him up, and they tipped him accordingly, which benefitted all of us, including the bussgirls whom Harry trained carefully himself and with whom he shared his tips. All in all he was a superb waiter. In fact, he had only one minor fault.

Being a night owl, he spent as much of his mornings as he possibly could sleeping soundly in his bed. We opened the Tea House for lunch at 12:00 noon sharp every day but Monday. Our customers, mainly downtown businessmen, had only limited time for lunch and had to be served promptly. It was therefore crucial for

Harry to be at the restaurant on time. To his credit he always was—but never before the last minute, by which time Eva and I were usually close to a nervous breakdown. Only when we spotted his little Volkswagon Beetle rounding the curve at 11.57 a.m. did we breath a sigh of relief.

At the end of each season Harry packed up his cameras and went on photographic safaris, often to San Francisco. It was the beginning of the Beatnik Era, and Harry spent a lot of time in Haight-Ashbury getting to know all the great characters of that time: Alan Ginsburg, Jack Kerouac, Henry Miller, Laurence Ferlinghetti, and many others. He photographed them pro bono, hoping to be able to cash in later, which he eventually did. At the time, however, he lived through his winters in San Francisco by relying on the previous summer's tips. And each spring he would show up in Vancouver dead broke, but very happy.

We were always pleased to have him back, yet we knew that he would eventually leave the restaurant business to focus on his photography. The parting came finally in 1957, when Harry moved to San Francisco. After a few hungry years there, in the early sixties, just when the war in Vietnam started heating up and the Americans were getting more and more involved, he got his big break. He was travelling in the Far East at the time, and *Time* and *Life* magazines were looking for someone to cover the events unfolding there. Being on the spot, he went to work for them, thus becoming the first Western photojournalist to enter Mao's China after the cultural revolution and before the Kissinger visit.

After many years of photojournalism, which took him to all the danger zones of the world, he moved to Phoenix, Arizona, where he raised a family with his beautiful Shanghai-born wife. When their two wonderful children flew the nest, they moved back to Vancouver. We remain very close to this day. Over the years our friendship has grown steadily deeper and stronger.

Shortly after Harry left us to go to San Francisco, we were joined by Bunu, our second waiter. He was a very handsome man who spoke four languages fluently with a heavy Hungarian accent, played the piano, and dabbled in photography. Descended from an old aristocratic Hungarian family (a fact he never brought to our attention), he sometimes acted in a bizarre manner that reminded us of the sort of foolishness lampooned in the many aristocrat jokes we'd heard while growing up in Hungary. Bunu had graduated from a prestigious hotel school in Switzerland. He was therefore far better trained than Harry, but unlike Harry he suffered from a serious lack of common sense.

When he first came to the Tea House, he drove up in a fully-restored Packard automobile, parked the car in our driveway, and slowly removed his deer-leather gloves and his driving goggles. He looked like a moviestar. Not surprisingly, all our female guests were smitten as they watched him entering the premises in his well tailored tuxedo. We were also pleased, thinking that he would add a touch of class to our establishment. The problem, we soon discovered, was that the male partners of the smitten ladies, who payed the bills and left the tips, were not eager to do either while their women were swooning over Bunu. And that was not the only problem.

**Bunu**,
assisted by Paula, serving tea to Steve and Eva,
Ferguson Point Tea House, c. 1958

**Eva**,
Indian Arm (near Vancouver), c. 1958

During Harry's tenure the Tea House had been considered a friendly, informal place with a distinctively rustic charm. Under Bunu's influence, however, it was transformed into a very formal and almost forbidding dining room, and the change—like Bunu's charm with the women—started to hurt our business. We responded by getting Bunu to remove his tuxedo and to park the Packard behind the Tea House. After that things hummed along nicely for a while, and we thought that all was well. But then Bunu decided to quit smoking. At first we encouraged him in this noble endeavour, but we soon discovered that it too was going to hurt our business.

Bunu arrived each morning without cigarettes in his pockets, determined to conquer his tobacco habit. By mid-afternoon, however, when the Tea House was filling up with our afternoon crowd, his craving for smokes became unbearable. Then, in desperation, he would order a cab from downtown to bring him a package. The one-way road around the park, plus the thirty-five cents for the cigarettes, plus the generous tip to the driver, came to five dollars: big money in those years. And this extravagant little scenario was played out each afternoon in full view of our customers, who began to wonder whether Bunu really needed the two-bit tips they usually gave for afternoon tea service.

Poor Bunu! He soon became the most poorly tipped waiter who ever worked in our restaurant, in spite of all his excellent training. Even so, he was a loyal employee who took great pride in his work, which I suppose explains why, after firing him on two occasions, we took him back both times. He tried very hard to please us, yet

**Ferguson Point Tea House**
Photograph by O.F. Landauer of Leonard Frank Photos,
Vancouver, Photo #30959

seldom succeeded. The same was perhaps true of his wives, of which he had four over the years, each one leaving him eventually. He worked with us for three seasons before returning to Switzerland, from where he would often phone to express his great yearning for Vancouver, Stanley Park, the Tea House, and Eva and me. I used to tease him about him being a majority shareholder in the Swiss telephone company: his ramblings over the phone lasted for hours sometimes and must have cost him a fortune. He is still living on the shores of the beautiful Lake Geneva teaching Yoga. We met him for the last time in 1987 in Montreux, where we discovered that he had exchanged his smoking habit for an addiction to alcohol. He had also hung on to his aristocratic eccentricity: when we met he was wearing non-matching socks of hideous colours.

After Bunu left, we had the good fortune to hire Ernie, another excellent headwaiter. Formerly a dining room steward on the CPR ships that provided regular Transatlantic service between Montreal and Liverpool, he was an Englishman who taught us plenty of Cockney slang, much of it in the form of rhyming ditties. Ernie, who had received excellent training on the boats, was methodical, and very loyal to us during his tenure at the Tea House, which was longer than that of either of his two predecessors. The only thing we didn't like about him was the way he went about getting bigger and better tips. On slow days, when he had the opportunity to engage his customers in a little private banter, he would tell them sob stories about his wintertime blues on unemployment insurance and explain how tough it was for him to provide food for his wife and his seven children. He would also blame the large number of his children on his lack of prosperity: since they had no money for TV or other entertainment, and since they had to snuggle together just to keep warm in their poorly heated dwelling, well, one thing led to another and they tended to have a new baby each year. I should perhaps add here that Eva and I ended up being god-parents to seven of them!

In spite of this connection, we have lost track of Ernie and his family. But we will always remember him fondly, especially for one memorable gesture which earned him our everlasting gratitude. Soon after we sold our business in 1964, we sailed to Europe on the *Empress of Canada*, one of those CPR ships that Ernie had served on before coming to the Tea House. As soon as he got wind of our plans, he notified his former colleagues there, that we were to receive special treatment. We got the surprise of our lifetime when we received a royal welcome from the crew and a complimentary upgrade from second to first class accommodation. Each evening we enjoyed the best table in the dining room, and when we returned to our stateroom we found fresh flowers and delicious chocolates. Thank you very much again, dear Ernie!

The other Tea House employee who must be mentioned here is Jimmy, the young Chinese cook I had hired in 1961, three years before we sold the business. Eva was all for my hiring kitchen help, since she knew that my heavy workload in the kitchen was taking a toll on my health, but she had reservations about my hiring a Chinese cook. She had no racial prejudices herself. Her opposition came strictly from the business point of view.

We had, she reasoned, built ourselves up as a European establishment. An oriental cook in the kitchen would not appeal to our clientele, some of whom, Eva felt, were racists. In the end, however, we decided to take the risk.

A very young-looking Chinese fellow answered my ad, yet he slouched like an old man. During the interview I could hardly understand his English. Even so, I decided to try him out, and I've never regretted doing so. The minute Jimmy changed and put on his white uniform his whole personality and bearing changed: he straightened up, becoming a head taller, and he moved quickly. Within no time he had mastered our routine and proved that he was loyal and reliable. I was therefore able to leave the kitchen in his hands when things slowed down, and when we got really busy, we two became a superb team, able to keep up with the maddest rush. Eva was soon calling him my number one son.

By the time we hired Jimmy, in 1961, Eva and I had long given up trying to keep the Tea House open all year round. Initially we had thought that we could stay open, but as the bright days of summer and autumn gave way to rain, drizzle and fog, people simply stopped coming to Stanley Park. Frustrated by the lack of clientele, Eva suffered a nervous breakdown, and our family doctor recommended a long winter holiday in a warm climate. At first I was reluctant to agree, but as the years passed we both got used to closing the Tea House after the Thanksgiving weekend and spending the rest of the winter on a beach in Mexico.

This idyllic pattern ended suddenly when I got hepatitis in Puerto Vallarta. Because of its infectious nature, this disease prevented me from working in the kitchen at the restaurant. I was quarantined in total isolation, which gave me plenty of time to think about the future. And as I thought, I slowly came to realize what my darling Eva had been telling me for years, namely, that there was no future for us in this business. We had been spending most of our hard-earned money on our winter holidays, and the liquor laws banning the sale of alcohol in Stanley Park effectively prevented us from earning more. And now, because of my quarantine, we had had to hire two persons to replace me. As a result, although Eva was still working ten-hour shifts, we had started losing money.

We sold the Tea House that summer, which was not an easy task, since the Parks Board insisted on making it clear to any prospective buyer, first, that no value could be attached to goodwill and, second, that they reserved the right to cancel the lease if the purchasers failed to maintain the good reputation established by us. In the end, we did find buyers. The new owners, a maitre'd and a short order cook, took over on July 1st 1964. One of the conditions of the sale, however, was that the Tea House would retain its employees. Having purchased CPR tickets to leave Vancouver on July 4th for Montreal, where we would be boarding the *Empress of Canada* to sail to Liverpool, we were rather disturbed when, on July 2nd, our whole staff, led by Ernie and Jimmy, showed up at our West End motel room and told us that they had walked out—unwilling and unable to work for their new bosses. Their loyalty to us was touching, but it threatened to scuttle the sale of the Teahouse. Fortunately, after a long night session, all of them went back to work the next day, saving us an embarrassment—not to mention a potential law-suit. Thank you dear friends.

We left Vancouver on July 4th as scheduled, rode the Canadian Pacific Railway to Montreal and boarded our ship for Liverpool. This was our first trip back to Europe and, since we knew that we would probably not be able to return again soon, we resolved to make the best of it while trying to stay within our rather limited budget. Using Frommer's *Europe on $ 5.00 a Day* as our bible, we had a wonderful time travelling from England to France, then on to Belgium, Holland, Germany, Denmark, and Switzerland. We made it to Vienna in time for my mother-in-law's seventy-second birthday.

From Vienna we attempted a short side-trip to Budapest, where most of Eva's family still lived. We went to the Canadian Embassy one day and asked one of the officers whether it would be safe for us to travel to Hungary. He very enthusiastically said yes. Hungary, he felt, was the most open society within the Eastern Block, its prevailing ideology known as "Goulash Communism." He had had a great time there a little while before, in Budapest. When I reminded him that we were not native-born Canadians like him but ex-Hungarian nationals who had left the country illegally, he did not seem to see any problem. When I emphasized that our Canadian passports listed our birthplace as Budapest, he suggested that we might do well to register with the Canadian Embassy in Vienna before leaving for Hungary, giving our return dates. He also recommended visiting the British Embassy in Budapest (Canada at that time did not have diplomatic ties with Hungary) and register there too. Then I asked him whether he would be able to help us if we got detained for any reason. His attitude changed immediately. "If you want guarantees, I cannot give you any," he said abruptly. "Maybe you should not go at this time."

Undaunted, Eva worked hard to contact by phone the relatives who had helped her in her early teens, but Directory Information denied any knowledge of their existence. Then one afternoon, after we had pretty much given up hope of connecting with her relatives, when Eva was window-shopping the Mariahilfer Strasse, she looked up and saw a very familiar face moving towards her. It was her eldest cousin Leslie. That chance encounter, in a city of two million people, with someone who was living behind the Iron Curtain seemed totally surreal. It turned out that Leslie, being an expert on shipping, was on his way to Germany, sent there on a trade misson by his Communist bosses.

We immediately noticed that he was not alone. A group of four or five men surrounded him. After the hugs and kisses we sensed that Leslie was very nervous and uncomfortable. He avoided introducing Eva to his companions, who must have been members of the Hungarian Secret Police. After a very short and strained conversation, during which Leslie tried desperately to avoid any reference to his relationship with Eva (and the secret police kept urging him to move on), Eva managed to give him a place and a time for a meeting, hoping against hope that he would be able to come unescorted.

When we arrived at the Opern Kaffee (Coffeehouse at the Opera) the next afternoon, Leslie had only one of the men sitting with him. Our meeting was very brief, but we did manage to learn that Leslie's family, including Eva's favorite Aunt Anna, was well. We also found out that Leslie's group was leaving that evening for Germany by rail and would return in four days, arriving at Vienna's Westbahnhof (Western Railway Station) at 12:45 p.m. After changing trains, they would be departing for Budapest. This latter information was written on a note that Leslie pressed into Eva's hand while they were embracing.

Four days later Eva and I waited in an upstairs balcony overlooking the main arrival area of the train station. Next to us stood two men in trench coats conversing in Hungarian. Obviously they were oblivious to us, as they were freely discussing their strategy about the reception they had planned for the trade group. They mentioned Leslie's name and suggested that he should get special attention because on his previous visit he had met with a suspicious couple who spoke Hungarian and were either Canadian or American Jews. What happened next could have been directed by Alfred Hitchcock.

A group of eight to ten men descended from the Hamburg Express. We recognized the four secret policemen and Leslie's escort from the Opern Kaffee. As they entered the big arrival hall, four groups of two men each moved in on them from the four corners of the station. The two men in trenchcoats also joined them. We tried to get to Leslie, but did not want to get him into trouble. All I managed to do was grab his suitcase, which I carried for him to the Budapest Express. As I boarded that train, a new engine was attached, giving our car a little lurch. Worried that the train was leaving

with me on board minus my Canadian passport, I pan-
icked, dropped the suitcase, and jumped off the train.
Eva, who was standing on the platform, was able to grab
Leslie's hand and say a brief goodbye. So much for the
"Goulash Communism" of Hungary.

A few days after our adventures in Vienna, we
travelled to Italy, the French Riviera, and the Spanish
Costa Brava. After that we journeyed back to Paris and
then England, where we caught *The Empress of Canada*
for its last Atlantic crossing of the year. In the course of
four-and-a-half wonderful months on the continent, we
spent the proceeds from the sale of the Tea House to the
last penny. It was an unforgettable adventure that
allowed us to see the sights of Western Europe that had
been denied to us in our youth. Although our future was
extremely shaky, we had no regrets.


When we returned to Vancouver, Eva acted on her long-
standing desire for a career in real estate. She maintained
that the effort that went into selling a dessert after a meal
was equal to the effort that went into selling a house,
while the rewards were quite different. She later con-
ceded that her theory had some faulty logic. My plan for
the future was based on my experience in the restaurant
business, where I had encountered some terrible
salesmanship on the part of my suppliers. Thinking I
could do better, I tried to offer them my services as a
consultant and as a sales-representative. They very politely ushered me into their inner sanctums, but after
hearing me out, every one of them rejected me. The
reason they gave was that, at the age of forty-four, I was

too old for the job. What they wanted was a twenty-four-year-old university graduate with long years of sales experience.

Once that door was closed, I decided to follow in the footsteps of my wife, who had enrolled in a real estate course. We both started in the spring of 1965. By the time summer came around she'd already sold four houses, while I was still pounding the pavement trying to get a start in the commercial end of the business. It took me a full year to make my first sale. That was a very long year. I was eaten by self-doubt and plagued by the idea that I had made the wrong career move. Eva, however, stood by me, encouraging me not to give up and helping me to resist the temptation to return to working for wages as a chef or souchef. By 1966 the ice was broken, and for the next twenty-four years I never looked back. I loved the business, enjoyed making deals, meeting people from all walks of life, shooting the breeze with my colleagues, and living life to the fullest.

I didn't even think of retiring from real estate until one day in 1989, when I was leafing through a magazine at a doctor's office and came upon an article dealing with retirement. It explored the fear that most professionals have of dealing with finances and suggested how they could deal with the leisure time that would fall into their laps after they quit working. It also dealt with all those would-be retirees who were putting off the decision, perhaps until it was too late to smell the roses. Attached to the article was a sample net worth statement of the kind you fill out when you approach your friendly neighbourhood banker for a loan or a mortgage. I tore out that page from the magazine, took it home, and filled in the blanks. The results screamed at me: Quit now before it is too late!

I was sixty-nine years old, with my 70th birthday just around the corner. I had already had my third arterial by-pass operation. My surgeon was warning me to quit smoking before he had to amputate my right leg. My work habits, incidentally, had made me so addicted to smoking that I had to light up before picking up the phone to talk to clients, before and after writing an offer to purchase or sell, and before and after having a cup of coffee. Realizing that I would soon be dead if I didn't quit working, I decided to retire. When I told Eva, she did not believe me at first, but I soon had her full support.

She also supported my decision to quit smoking, which I made at the same time as my decision to retire, by quitting herself. That was one of the bravest things she ever did for me. She had started smoking at the age of fourteen and, over the years, had enjoyed it a great deal. She knew, of course, that it could kill her one day. Her response to that possibility was simply, "So be it: we all have to die sooner or later." Yet as soon as our family doctor warned her that even second-hand smoke would be dangerous to my health, she quit without hesitation.

Our retirement years were rather quiet and mostly spent in Vancouver. We did, however, travel a good deal, and several of those trips stand out in my memory, especially our returns to Hungary. The first of these took place late in the summer of 1976 when we travelled once again to Europe, this time with an organized tour that included a cruise of the Greek Islands, brief visits to Athens and Istanbul, one week's stay in Dubrovnik, and four nights in London. Since Budapest was so close to Dubrovnik, we were able to exchange our four nights in London for three nights in the Hungarian capital. By this time we had heard first hand from friends and relatives that conditions had improved considerably. And we were curious to see for ourselves what had become of our homeland during the thirty-one years since we crossed over the border into Austria.

In Dubrovnik we met two young secretaries from Budapest whom the state had granted a short vacation on the Dalmatian coast. They emphatically confirmed the stories about the improved conditions in Hungary and told us about a new literary cabaret where the actors made fun of the Communist system and laughed at "Holy Mother Russia." They warned us, though, that the small theatre was sold out for more than a year in advance, and that we would probably not understand some of the satire performed there. Assured by their words, we flew from Dubrovnik to Budapest and checked into the grand dame of all Budapest hotels, the Hotel & Spa Gellert. A tip of ten US dollars to the concierge got us the best seats in the house at the above-mentioned cabaret that night. The satire, we discovered, was not that difficult to understand. The only thing we could not figure out was why the Communist authorities tolerated it at all. We got the answer to this question from Gyuri, who had served as our witness at our marriage years before. The cabaret, he explained, had only 250 seats, and the party functionaries usually

booked half of them. Thus the cabaret provided a very
small percentage of the population with a means of vent-
ing steam without really threatening the social order. In
fact the cabaret provided the authorities with an effective
means of placating the West: "Look", the cabaret
seemed to say, "how democratic we are, how unafraid of
criticism." And whenever the Soviet authorities came to
visit, the cabaret could easily be closed.

Since Eva and I had resolved not to contact Eva's relatives this time around, we had plenty of time to explore
the city. Most of the bridges destroyed during the war
had been rebuilt by now. Yet, in spite of these familiar
landmarks, we felt lost most of the time, mainly because
practically all the streets had been renamed. Whenever
we wanted to find a certain address, we had to ask
directions from elderly people, who still remembered
the old street names. Just imagine if you returned to
Vancouver after thirty years and found Robson street
renamed People's Democracy Street or Georgia Street
called Stalin Boulevard. To add to our confusion, even
the familiar statues in the parks and public squares were
switched around. Our overall impression of the city was
not favourable: aside from a few tourist districts and the
occasional grand old apartment, the buildings in the city
were crying out for basic repairs. Because all housing was
state owned and the rents were ridiculously low, main-
tenance was completely neglected. Almost everywhere
we went the plaster was falling, the elevators did not
work, and the plumbing was a mess.

One day we boarded a sightseeing bus with a group
of German and British tourists. Our guide, a young
woman, spoke excellent German and English, but she

**Elizabeth Bridge**, Budapest

refused to speak Hungarian. We drove from Heroes
Square (no name change here) along one of the main
roads of the capital, which in my youth was called
Andrassy Boulevard. As we passed No. 60, which both
the Gestapo and the Hungarian Secret Police had used
for detaining, torturing and executing political
opponents, our guide mentioned nothing about this
dark history. When I asked her about her silence she
pretended not to hear me.

While it had been amazingly easy to enter the country, leaving for London was more complicated. As we
made our way through the airport, police state tactics
were everywhere in full view. We had to go through a
number of control stations, showing our identification,
emptying our pockets to show we had no more than
200 forints (100 forints were worth one CDN dollar at
that time), and submitting to body searches. Needless to
say, the authorities we dealt with at every turn were
unsmiling, unfriendly, and heavily armed. That farewell,
combined with a very rocky flight to London on a
Russian built Tupolev aircraft, eliminated any desire we
might have had for another visit in the near future.

In 1984, however, after both Eva and I had been diag-
nosed with the beginnings of osteo-arthritis, our family
doctor recommended some mineral bath therapy. Our
Hungarian friends and Eva's relatives were all raving
about the Spas of Hungary, which have been celebrated
throughout the world from the time the Turks occupied
most of Central Hungary. So, lured by the healing waters
of the spas, we returned to Hungary once again. This

time we chose the Hotel Thermal, located at the north end of St. Margaret's Island in a beautiful park-like setting where no vehicle traffic except public transportation was allowed.

Since Eva and I had agreed to get in touch with relatives this time around, I contacted my Uncle Maximillian's only daughter, Vera, whom I had not seen in forty years. Ours was a very sad reunion. The once lively, fashion-conscious young girl had turned into a lethargic, broken old woman. She was living with her equally lethargic, sickly, old husband in one of those state-owned, neglected, crumbling apartment complexes. The paint in their apartment was peeling, the plumbing needed repair, and the street entrance reeked of an unpleasant mixture of urine, garbage, and stale pipe tobacco. I was sad to learn that my vivacious, pretty cousin had ended up this way.

On the brighter side, I was pleased to see signs of "Goulash Communism" at work. The new leader of Hungary, Janos Kadar, had been handpicked by the Soviets after the 1956 revolution, the one suppressed by Russian tanks. But Kadar had liberal ideas (unlike many of the other leaders of the Eastern Bloc). He carefully steered Hungary towards a more open society and a free market economy. Always fond of slogans, he declared, "All those who are not against us are with us," meaning that the suspicious attitude of the old Party hacks had been replaced by a more generous spirit. The more relaxed atmosphere made for a good visit. The baths were wonderful, the food was good and, by Canadian standards, very inexpensive. Wherever we went, a little tipping got us excellent service.

**Parliament Buildings,**
Budapest, where, until the Communists fell in 1989, free
speech was very seldom practiced

Several days into our visit I remembered that one of my real estate clients in Vancouver had asked me to do him a little favour in Budapest. He then handed me a paper in Russian script and told me it was a non-prescription natural remedy against his worsening arthritis. To the best of his knowledge it was available in Hungary. Would I mind buying some for him during my stay? Since the Hotel Thermal had a resident medical staff, I showed the paper to the doctor assigned to us. She looked at it carefully for a moment, then blurted out, "This is in Russian!" Yes, I said, I knew that. To make a long story short, of the 400-odd employees of the hotel, I could not find one person who was able to read it, despite the fact that for the past 38 years the Russian language was compulsory in all schools. After almost two weeks of searching, I finally found a pharmacist down-town who was up to the task. So much, I thought with pleasure, for the dominance of Soviet culture!

Before we left Budapest I made good on the promise I had made to try to locate and visit my father's grave in the Jewish Cemetery. I had been there a couple of times in my youth after my maternal grandparents passed away. As I approached the gates this time, I had an eerie feeling. The place seemed to be totally deserted. At the gatekeeper's residence I saw a note taped to the door giving a phone number in case anyone wished information, but there were no telephones anywhere. The gate to the cemetery, however, was open, so I wandered in. As I remembered from my youth, near the entrance were the graves and the great mausoleums of all the prominent Jewish authors, poets, playwrights, politicians, actors and captains of industry and commerce. All of these were now in ruins, vandalized, graffiti-ridden, over-grown with weeds: a veritable wasteland, where only the buzzing of the insects could be heard that warm May morning.

After looking for a while, and realizing the futility of trying to locate my father's grave in that wasteland, I walked over to the neighbouring Catholic cemetery, hoping someone there could help me me or at least let me use their telephone. I told the custodians there about my search in the dilapidated cemetery. They listened with great sympathy and then asked me very politely, whether I was of the Jewish faith? As they put it, the question is virtually impossible to translate. The Hungarian language has a way of addressing a stranger or a respected elder that is so polite it borders on the ridiculous. Translated verbatim, the question I was asked would sound something like this: "Are you pleased to be of the Jewish faith, Sir?" I had a great desire to respond, "No, dear people, I am not at all pleased, but let's face it: that is what I am whether you or I or anybody else likes it or not!" Instead, I merely nodded and listened as they kindly explained to me that there were two Jewish cemeteries and gave me directions to the one I had yet to visit. That cemetary proved to be much better maintained than the other, so, with the help of Eva's cousin Ervin, I was able to locate my father's grave. Although my mother told me she had paid for the perpetual care of father's plot, it took half an hour to dig enough dirt away from the gravestone to read the inscription: FREUND, GUSZTÁV 1872-1944. Yes, my family name was orig-inally Freund.

**Steve and Eva,**
on an Alaskan cruise,
1970

**Eva**
in Marakesh, 1979

Just before we left Budapest, an unpleasant incident spoiled what had otherwise been a near-perfect vacation. Walking on one of the grand boulevards, we passed by one of the state-owned food markets. The scent of the food (rather than the meager window display) prompted us to enter the store. As we had full board at our hotel, the idea of buying groceries had never occurred to us up to that time. Now that we found ourselves in a grocery store, however, we started piling into our shopping basket all kinds of items which we had not seen or tasted since our youth. How pleasing that was! It was pure nostalgia-hoarding.

Just after Eva had exchanged one huge loaf of country-style bread for another smaller one, a male voice yelled in Hungarian: "Put that bread back where it belongs!" Pretending to neither hear nor understand, we continued to make our way towards the cashier. When the man yelled at us again, a woman in the crowd said, "Leave them alone. Can't you see they are foreigners? They don't know our rules!" "They are no foreigners!" the man yelled back at the woman. "They are a couple of stinking Jews!" He kept making these antisemitic remarks while we paid for our purchases. Even after we left the store, he pursued us, shouting, "Rotten Jew Bastards!" This time I turned around to give him an answer, but he made a very fast getaway. His brand of overt racism was officially prohibited by the Hungarian government, so I could have reported him to the authorities. Our relatives, however, discouraged us from doing this, and since we were leaving the next morning, we did not pursue the matter.

When we returned to Hungary five years later, in 1989, we checked into the Hotel Thermal once again for more Spa treatment. By this time there was great euphoria in the air. Gorbachev was in power and the Communist government of Hungary was allowing free passage to East Germans wanting to join their brothers in West Germany. The first cracks in the hated Berlin wall were appearing everywhere. As we entered the country, for example, the custom's inspector, noticing that we were Hungarian born, could hardly contain his pleasure over recent events. Ignoring our English-speaking fellow passengers, he sang odes to us about his newly won freedoms.

One week later Eva planned a luncheon get-together with her whole family at one of the newly-opened, privately-owned restaurants. We made a reservation in person and were assured that we would be taken care of in grand style. Upon arriving at the appointed time, we noticed that the restaurant was quite busy, so we asked the headwaiter whether they remembered our reservation for eight persons. He looked us straight in the eye and said, "There are no reservations taken here by me or anybody else. It is first come, first served!" We started protesting and told him that we had personally seen the manager entering our names into the reservation book. He then said with a sneer, "Can't you understand plain Hungarian? We . . . do . . . not . . . take . . . reservations. Besides, he added with an ironic smile, "We've already had the pleasure of knowing your kind of people."

Under the Communists, as I noted earlier, such racist remarks could have landed the man a prison sentence. Now, thanks to the collapse of the Berlin

Wall, he was free to state openly that he hated Jews—proof positive that freedom has its costs. Those costs were evident again later during a televised soccer game between Austria and Hungary, where a giant Swastika was unfurled from the grandstand and left hanging during the whole game. To this day, Hungary has not renounced its antisemitism. After the last elections in Austria, when Jorg Haider's neo-nazis became part of the ruling coalition government, all of Europe condemned the Austrians. The only vocal supporters of Haider were the Hungarian parlamentarians.

Not all of the trips we took after retiring were to Hungary. In September of 1994, for example, we went on an unforgettable cruise of the South Seas, along with many other Canadians. Except for the Maritimes, all regions were well represented, including *la Belle Province*, home to approximately two dozen of our fellow passengers. One of them, a certain Jean-Paul B., a manufacturer from Quebec City, I got to know fairly well. Our first meeting took place on the promenade deck, where both of us did our mile walk (five times around the deck) each day. Having noticed his t-shirt decorated with the fleur-de-lis, I greeted him by saying, "*Bon jour mon confrère Canadien!*" He smiled, and we struck up a conversation during which he complimented me, an "anglo" from British Columbia, for speaking French. His English, I have to confess, was far superior to my high-school French. From then on we met daily, doing our exercises together, exchanging a little small talk, yet carefully avoiding all political discussion.

On one occasion, our captain invited all the Canadians on board to a special Canadian Thanksgiving

**Steve and Eva,**
1992

celebration. We sang "O Canada," "Alouette," "Frère Jacques," we played an all-Canadian quiz-game, and we talked and swapped stories about the provinces and cities we hailed from. Everyone had a great time and felt proud to be Canadian. The only flaw in the evening was that no one from Quebec showed up. Many in our group said *Let them go to hell! Who needs them?* These comments, not to mention the absence of the Quebec contingent, made me feel very sad. Next morning at breakfast I stopped by Jean Paul's table and said, "We all missed you and your fellow Quebecers at our Thanksgiving feast. Why didn't you come?" Looking at me long and hard with very sad eyes, he finally spoke up. "Do you know the motto of our province? *Je me souviens*. I remember!" And then he burst into a long tirade, listing all the perceived grievances stretching all the way from the battle on the Plains of Abraham to the composition of the provincial school boards and the federal immigration policies which reduce the number of francophones in a sea of anglophones.

I listened and could not get a word in edgewise. Finally I blurted out, "Our Prime Minister is a French Canadian, so is the Minister of Finance and the Governor General. Even the Leader of Her Majesty's Loyal Opposition (Lucien Bouchard at the time) hails from Quebec. If we anglos can live with that, why can't you?" His answer was another "*Je me souviens*," meaning that Jean Chrétien and his ministers were traitors and *vendus*." Remember the repatriation of the Constitution," he continued, "and the humiliation of Meech Lake!" I told him only, "Please think twice before you file for a divorce. You must remember that in all divorces it is the

children, yours and mine, who suffer the consequences."
This was my last conversation with Jean Paul. *Adieu,
mon ami.* You made me, as you would say, *très triste,*
especially since within the next year, your attitude would
come perilously close to breaking apart the Canada that
has been such a wonderful haven for Eva and me, and so
many others like us.

Now there is a day I will never forget: October 30, 1995:
referendum day in Quebec. The emotions of all
Canadians had been going up and down like a yo-yo for
the preceding few weeks. Would the unthinkable happen? Would Jacques Parizeau push all the right buttons?
Would Jean Chrétien finally pull his head out of the
sand? If we did separate, how would we divide all our
marbles fairly and squarely, including the national debt?
Are the threats of separation deplorable scare tactics
manipulated by unscrupulous bankers on Bay Street, or
well-thought-out economic theories forecasting gloom
and doom? Is it too late? Have we all gone mad? Is anyone willing to listen to reason? What will happen to all
our values and all our valuables: our country, our stocks
and bonds, our homes, our real estate, our loonie? Will
our friendly neighbour to the south gobble us up one
by one, province by province? These and other such
questions had given us sleepless nights for weeks.

On the fateful day of the referendum we had tickets
to the opera *Faust,* quite appropriately, I thought;
Jacques Parizeau always struck me as Mephisto incar-
nate. We thought we might as well have one more good
night on the town before Canada broke up. At 5:30 p.m.

Pacific Standard Time, half an hour after the Quebec polls closed, we went out for dinner. On the way to the restaurant we listened to the early results on the car radio. The news was not good. It seemed that the separatists would cakewalk away from Canada. Not wanting to contemplate that thought, we turned off the radio.

After dinner we walked over to the Queen Elizabeth Theatre. It was 7:55 p.m. when we took our seats. We were listening to the orchestra tuning up when all of a sudden, like a giant tidal wave, voices rose in crescendo from the audience. In a few seconds everyone was standing, eyes fixed on the electronic translation screen above the stage and singing "O Canada!" The orchestra joined in a minute later. The final results were flashing on the screen. By a very minuscule margin, reason had won out this time! My relief was diminished somehat when I recalled Rene Levesque's comments when the separatists lost the 1980 referendum: "*A la prochaine, mes amis.*"[3] Even so, that evening at the Queen Elizabeth Theatre was a joyful occasion—so beautiful, so spontaneous, so filled with emotion. It was something to remember forever!

It was certainly on my mind in September of 1996, as Eva and I travelled to the Maritimes to celebrate the anniversary of our arrival in Halifax with a cruise along the Eastern seaboard. On the clear, windy morning of September 25th—forty-eight years, to the day, after we first set foot on Canadian soil—*The Royal Princess* slowly eased into Halifax Harbour. I was on the top deck looking at Pier 21. John Nolan, our wonderful escort, stood next to me. The banner which had greeted us in

3. Till the next time, my friends.

1948 was no longer there, but I could clearly remember how moved I had been by those words: WELCOME HOME TO CANADA. I told John about how touched we had been, and how those memories and emotions were taking hold of me again. In our day of sightseeing, we visited the Citadel and learned about the great disaster in Halifax Harbour where thousands upon thousands of Haligonians lost their lives. That evening at dinnertime John came over to our table and, without saying a word, placed a book next to me. *Pier 21*, by Trudy Duivenvoorden Mitic and J.P. Lebanc, told the story of that blessed place where most twentieth-century immigrants first set foot on Canadian soil before proceeding to change the face of Canada, forever. Our hard-working escort, by choosing to use his free time to find us the perfect gift, had given yet another reason to be grateful for our gentle, new country. Upon opening the book, I discovered that John had dedicated it to Eva and me. Thank you, John. And thank you, Canada!

# EPILOGUE

Yet each man kills the thing he loves,
By each let this be heard.
Some do it with a bitter look,
Some with a flattering word.
The coward does it with a kiss,
The brave man with a sword!

—Oscar Wilde

August 27, 2000
Vancouver, B.C.

My Dearest Eva,

I felt drained, devastated and lost as I stood over your casket and looked down into the terrible emptiness of your open grave four days ago on that beautiful but bitter day in August. For us it was always August. We met for the first time fifty-eight years ago on the twentieth day of August, 1942. We got married almost three years later on the fifteenth of August, 1945. We left the Old World for our new home in Canada on the 16th of August, 1948. Then, a little over two weeks ago, on the eighth of August, I accidentally drove you to your death. And two weeks later, on the twenty-third of August, I buried you, my dearest treasure, my best friend, my partner, my wife. Oh, how I wish you had survived rather than me.

Thinking back to the day of the accident, I remember that I had wanted to treat you to dinner at the water's edge on Granville Island. We were pleased, when we got

Left: **Eva**, 1955

157

there, to find an open parking spot in the row right next to the water. As the nose of our vehicle approached the railing, I pressed my foot down on what I thought was the brake, but my foot must have slipped and hit the gas. All I know for sure is that in an instant our vehicle was plunging into the water. My survivor's instinct took over immediately. I unbuckled myself and somehow managed to open the door. Next thing I knew I was swimming on the surface.

Four men were soon swimming around me and trying to help me to land. I yelled at them: "Please forget me! I am OK. Try to get my wife out PLLEEAASE! I beg you." "Where was she sitting?" they asked. "In the front passenger seat, of course!" I said, thinking to myself "what a stupid question!" After one of the men dove down and resurfaced, he said, "She's not there." "Please, please find her. Please, please." I kept saying as two husky paramedics pulled me out of the water, put me on a gurney and drove me in an ambulance to Vancouver Hospital Emergency. Along the way they asked lots of questions about relatives, or friends, or any next of kin they should notify. I must have been in a shock, as I finally blurted, "Elizabeth and Earl and Adele Moss." I could not for the life of me remember their telephone numbers. Even so, all three of them were by my bedside in the hospital.

When I asked about you repeatedly, wanting to know how you were, the answers I received were guarded. You were breathing, they said, but you needed a respirator. Yes, the doctors were working on you, but

Right: **Eva's** legacy at the front entrance

I should not build up much hope. Around midnight, Earl and Elizabeth guided me to your gurney. You were breathing heavily. Your eyes opened up from time to time, but the nurse told me you were not going to live. As you slipped slowly away, I begged you "Please, stay with me. Don't abandon me." Soon, however, you were gone. My stupid mistake had cost me my greatest treasure, my wife.

Today I am sitting in our favorite bay window trying to listen to our favourite tunes. At the moment it's "*Noche de ronda, que triste pasa en mi corazon,*"[4] sung by Elvira Rios, whose smoky voice is accompanied by guitars and violins. It tears my heart out, but I can't stop. I'm crying and sobbing, wondering if you will ever be able to forgive me. Tomorrow I will play Edith Piaff singing "*Je ne regret rien,*" but as for me, believe me, my dearest Eva, I do regret very much!"

More than that, though, I feel deep gratitude for the wonderful fifty-five years we enjoyed together. Now that you are gone from this world, my dearest, let me dedicate this book to you. I feel convinced that your desire for privacy has passed, and I believe that you will smile down from heaven and accept this memorial to our love.

Your ever-loving husband,
Steve

4. Night of the fiesta—how sadly it touches my heart.